# A YEAR STRAIGHT

## CONFESSIONS OF A BOY-CRAZY
## LESBIAN BEAUTY QUEEN

ELENA AZZONI

SEAL PRESS

# A YEAR STRAIGHT

*Confessions of a Boy-Crazy Lesbian Beauty Queen*

Copyright © 2011 by Elena Azzoni

Published by
Seal Press
A Member of the Perseus Books Group
1700 Fourth Street
Berkeley, California

Library of Congress Cataloging-in-Publication Data

Azzoni, Elena, 1975-
   A year straight : confessions of a boy-crazy lesbian beauty queen / Elena Azzoni.
      p. cm.
   ISBN 978-1-58005-361-7
   1. Azzoni, Elena, 1975- 2. Lesbians—United States—Biography. 3. Lesbians—Relations with heterosexuals. 4. Man-woman relationships. I. Title.
   HQ75.4.A99A3 2011
   306.76'63092—dc23
   [B]
                                        2011019604
9  8  7  6  5  4  3  2  1

Cover design by Briar Levit
Interior design by Domini Dragoone
Printed in the United States of America
Distributed by Publishers Group West

*In order to respect the privacy of individuals mentioned in the book, the author has changed names and in some cases created composite characters.*

## Dedication

For Inanna

And for every single woman attracted to men,
may the force be with you.

# Contents

# CHAPTER ONE

# The Adjustment

**T**he ladies' locker room was abuzz with women racing to change, so they could place their mats up front near Him, The Yoga Teacher. The faint guttural chants of kirtan rock star Krishna Das played on repeat over the hum of hair dryers in an effort to calm our New York nerves. But there was no sign of Zen around there. There was, rather, a subtle current of competition. I snuck peeks at the other women as they pranced around in lacy thongs, sifting frantically through their lockers for yoga pants, lotion, and hair ties. With my long hair and lipstick, I fell under the gaydar and was free to gaze. It had been years since I'd been concerned with impressing a man, so as the other women primped and groomed, I rolled my eyes, relieved to have no interest whatsoever in competing in *that* particular pageant.

ONE MONTH EARLIER . . .

"Let's have a big round of applause for all of our contestants!"

The spotlight is blinding, and a bead of sweat makes its way down my temple in agonizing slow motion, dissolving into my red-sequined evening gown. Standing ovation from a sold-out audience, more than three hundred in attendance. The Luna Lounge is over max capacity. The fire department told us so. Following four hours of grueling competition and eight laborious costume changes, it's time to determine the winner. We've performed our various talents, including a tranny boi band, my eighties retro jazz dance, and someone giving birth to a doll. Likewise, we've endured the ever-dreaded swimsuit competition and the nerve-racking interview segment, in which at least one contestant routinely flops. Backstage is littered with wigs, glitter, and silicone accoutrements of varying colors, lengths, and girths. It looks like a tornado passed through a sex toy shop.

"And the winner is . . . "

Murray Hill places the sash over my shoulder and the tiara on my head. A fellow contestant hugs me, nearly knocking it off. I've won! I've won the crown! Journalists paw at me as my picture is snapped alongside the panel of celebrity judges. I smile and wave at the sea of screaming women. I am the new Miss Lez.

I'd resisted the pageant at first. After posing as a *Baywatch* babe in the premier issue of the lesbian calendar "I Heart Brooklyn Girls," my friends encouraged me to go for the crown.

"You can represent the calendar!"

My shy side battled my inner Carmen Electra. Ever since I could kick-ball-change, I'd been dancing in recitals, performing in plays, and mocking myself in my own comedic routines. I was no stranger to the stage, but I was ready to retire, done with the sleepless nights leading up to shows, where I'd bolt upright in a panic, wondering, *How did I get myself into this?* But I eat up the spotlight like a plate of baked ziti. I consoled myself, assuming the pageant would entail one week of performance anxiety followed by one humiliating night under bright lights, and then it'd be done. But I won.

The following weeks were a flurry of phone calls and emails initiating me into my new celesbian status. There were magazine and news interviews, photo requests, a stint on TV, and invites to elite social gatherings. At the climax of my success, I found myself in L.A., seated across from big-time producers, a finalist for a role on a grueling hit reality show. It was determined that I am not cut out for reality TV, which is probably for the best, for I am a homicidal (self-diagnosed) hypoglycemic. And there is no food on that show.

My limelight gradually faded to a low dim, and my life went back to normal. I'd go to work, hatch up new escape plans from my cubicle (*I should go to cosmetology school!*), head out to a lesbian bar, and attempt to return home early enough to pretend I'd get up for yoga the next day.

ON ONE QUITE ordinary evening, I took my time weaving through the crooked streets of the West Village on my way to meet up with friends. The layout of that neighborhood is drastically different from the rest of Manhattan, having come to life long before the grid. I got lost as usual. The cobblestone streets all started looking the same, and I was sure I was going in circles. After rounding several more corners, the pink glow of The Cubbyhole was my lighthouse in the fog. The windows perspired with body heat and the promise of a late-night make-out. The familiar scent of stale beer and cigarettes wafted over me as I squeezed past the butch bouncer smoking by the door.

"Good evening. Can I see your ID?"

I love being carded.

An eclectic mess of Christmas tree lights, paper lanterns, and leis, the ceiling of The Cubbyhole feels like it's caving in. The walls are plastered with Dolly Parton posters, and the jukebox caters to fans of both Rihanna and k. d. lang. I heard my name called from across the bar, waved to my crew camped out in the corner, and mimed drinking from a glass. As I strained to make eye contact with the bartender, someone recognized me from the pageant.

"Miss Lez!" She threw her arm around me and held up her phone to snap a shot of us together. She smelled good, as women usually do, like perfume and fruity shampoo. And then she planted a kiss on me. Click. I knew the picture would likely end up on the Internet somewhere, and I hoped my recent ex wouldn't come across it. It had been a few months since we'd split, and we were on amicable terms, so I didn't want her to think I'd simply found someone new. My claim of needing time for myself was true. Blue Moon in hand, I stealthily made my way over to my friends, dodging the already tipsy patrons. As the name implies, The Cubbyhole is cozy (or cramped, depending on my mood). Many a drink had been spilled on me there.

"So, which awe-inspiring, life-altering party is it gonna be tonight?" my friend TJ asked sarcastically. She'd just broken up with her psychology grad student girlfriend, claiming she felt like a patient. I'd argued that TJ could use a shrink. There were two lesbian parties scheduled for the same night. Taking into account recent breakups and new crushes, my friends weighed the options, casting their votes all at once:

"I refuse to go to Snapshot. Tami will be there flaunting her new twenty-two-year-old girlfriend."

"What about that new one in Brooklyn?"

"No way! Becca and Lisa are promoting it, and they didn't invite me to Fire Island this year."

"But Lola is bartending, and she has a crush me. You know what that means?"

"Free drinks!"

Even a city as big as New York gets really small when you're gay. Brooklyn won, as the less costly of the two boroughs, and everyone thought the British DJ was cute.

"Move it, dumbass." TJ got up and stepped over me. The bar was crowded for a Tuesday, and she liked to use the bathroom before it got busy with people getting busy in it. I knew her every move, as we'd been friends for what seemed like forever. We'd met in college, where I'd fallen in love with her gruff voice, and then her. Dating was not our calling, as we fought like two male betta fish tossed into a tiny tank, but we'd remained friends through the years, all the while driving each other nuts. She, the Ernie to my Bert, was full of harebrained ideas, always hungover, never on time, and a loyal, steadfast friend.

I nursed my beer and hummed along to Joan Jett blaring on the jukebox, substituting the *he*'s with *she*'s. "I saw her dancin' there by the record machine." TJ returned from the bathroom and downed the last of her drink.

"Ready for another night of high hopes and fruitless outcomes?" TJ asked, poking me in the ribs.

"You're on your own tonight," I said, pulling out my MetroCard. "I'm heading home so I can get up early for yoga tomorrow." I grabbed my bag and shot out of my chair to avoid the inevitable taunting.

"That's weak, Miss Lez. What kind of role model are you?"

"A lesbian one. I have to go feed my cat."

I was cat-sitting my ex-ex-girlfriend's cat, Kiki. By ex-ex, I mean her to be the ex before my more recent one. With Amy, enough time had passed that we could be friends, and therefore I could cat-sit. Kiki greeted me at my apartment door with a head-butt to my shin. I poured some organic, gluten-free, fair-trade, shade-grown, ovo-lacto-vegetarian cat food into her bowl and prepared a cheese plate for myself. I'm a big fan of food but quite lazy when it comes to cooking it. I maintain a sparse but specific stock of provisions: cheese, chocolate, brown rice, tea, ice cream, wine, and kale. On especially lazy days, I order pumpkin curry from To Be Thai.

I poured a glass of pinot noir and plopped myself down on my couch. Drinking wine alone never ceases to feel luxurious. Kiki, poised for the pounce, let out a squeak somewhere between a meow and a purr and jumped up to join me for reruns of *Sex and the City*. I fell asleep on the couch and dragged myself to bed at three.

My new alarm clock announced the abrupt arrival of morning. I'd requested it for Christmas from the L.L. Bean catalog as if I were ten again, though back then I'd have campaigned for the purple backpack with the signature reflective strip. I was determined to make early morning yoga a regular practice. The blaring alarm, reminiscent of the bell that announced the start and end of recess, was jarring enough to catapult the heaviest of sleepers out of bed.

Outside my building, a blast of humidity kick-started my step toward the air-conditioned subway. Ditmas Park, my Brooklyn neighborhood, just far enough from the city to still be affordable, is home to Jewish bakeries, Greek diners, ninety-nine-cent stores, a hippie co-op, and a Tibetan café. I'd moved to the area when my previous neighborhood, Lesbian Utopia Park Slope, became too crowded. I could no longer walk down the street without dodging dog walkers and double-wide, three-wheeled strollers. I swiped my Metro-Card along with the other early risers, mostly construction workers and hospital personnel. I savored my early morning ride. At 6:00 a.m., I even got a seat. Breezing through the easy-level Sudoku in the free daily *Metro,* I caught a glimpse of the man's paper in front of me. Lindsay Lohan and Samantha Ronson had been spotted shopping together in London again. I love a dose of juicy gossip—a small reward for getting up in time for yoga.

Once in the marble entryway of Eclipse Gym, I checked the clock and called the elevator to head up to the yoga studio. It wasn't the type of place I would normally seek out, being all brand-new and fancy, and a gym. I preferred the grungy, ivy-growing-up-the-walls type yoga studio, but since I worked nearby, I got a sweet corporate discount. Some of my coworkers had also fallen for the deal, and I would see them around now and then, though they mostly used the machines. Noah from sales ran ten miles per morning on the treadmill nearest the TV. He winked at me as I walked by. Like several other guys at work, he was determined to turn me.

After wrangling my hair into a knotty, haphazard bun, I made my way to class. I was nearly trampled as perfectly coiffed women scurried past me to the room. I calmly unrolled my mat in my favorite spot, back right corner by the window. On clear days, the sun would shine in on me during savasana. Also, I could look out the window rather than be distracted by the women around me, stretching, showing off their paper-thin Lululemon yoga pants. I'd seen them for sale in the gift shop and could have fed myself for a month on the cost of one pair. I preferred my black leggings and "I Heart NY" T-shirts. At five for $10 in Chinatown, I didn't worry about losing them somewhere between the gym, work, and home, which happened quite regularly.

In walked Dante, with his tattoos, Adidas pants, and freshly shaved head—a new age David Beckham. I stared at him along with the other women, but while they were imagining ungodly acts, I was admiring his goddess tattoos. Lakshmi wrapped around his left arm, pointing up to Shakti on tiptoe across his neck. He took his seat at the front of the room and placed his hands together in prayer. He flashed me a smile and I returned it, garnering the envy of several students in the room. Dante and I had become acquaintances when one day after class he had announced an event sponsored by my favorite chocolate company. There would be free chocolate. Naturally, I followed him out of the studio to get the details. He'd handed me his card, suggesting I email him for more information. And so we struck up a casual email correspondence, playful and perhaps a little flirtatious, but nothing for Miss

Lez to worry about. He was really funny, and I had fun being funny back. Generally speaking, I maintained a great rapport with men. Men made great friends, but I was not attracted to them. I had not so much as kissed a man in seven years, nor dated one in a decade, and had no expectation of doing either, barring a shift of tectonic plates.

"Ommmmm." I closed my eyes and placed my hands together, trying to make peace with my overactive mind. "Ommmmm." *Oh, I have to stop at New Morning for vitamin D after work.* "Ommmmm." *And fetch my sweater from the dry cleaner before they give it away.* "Ommmmm." *And call Sallie Mae to ask if I can lower my student loan payment.* "Ommmmm." Once into the flow of the poses, it was a little easier to let go, for it took all the concentration I had to balance in triangle or to breathe while doing a headstand. Yoga was a reprieve from my ever-productive, overanalyzing Virgo disposition, though it did require constant self-reminders throughout class. *Elena, just be!*

Halfway through class, while I was splayed out in pigeon pose, muttering a self-berating mantra at my tight hips, Dante approached me. I was equal parts enlightened and fed up. As the name implies, pigeon is an awkward pose, and it happens to be the most challenging for me. Sweating and silently swearing to myself, I felt him straddle the air around me and place his hands on my back. I surrendered to the weight of him pressing into me. *Okay, I can do this.* His warm breath inches from my ear, I eased deeper into the pose. At first I felt nothing but the usual throbbing of my hamstring and the release of my breath, opening, as we are taught, "to the edge." As the intensity increased, I stopped swearing to myself and cursed him out in my head instead. It's such a love-hate relationship with yoga teachers. I love them when they're draping a blanket over me at the end of class, but when they're pressing my arms backward as if in a vise, I have some unsettling thoughts. Leaning even more heavily into me, his heart beat against my back. My own heart, which was pounding at twice the rhythm of his, skipped a beat. Suddenly, I was acutely aware of his body touching mine, like I'd never been during any other yoga adjustment. Simultaneously suffocating and intrigued, I feared something might snap.

And then it did.

Out of a deep and dusty abyss stirred a strange sensation. I exhaled, which prompted Dante to press down even harder. I let out a whimper and he eased up. But the damage was done. I was drowning in a rush of desire. I couldn't tell which way was up, but I knew where he was, and it was on top of me. I wanted to turn around and tear into him, ripping his little yoga teacher tank top to shreds. I wanted to see *all* his tattoos. Oblivious that he had just pushed Miss Lez's libido button, he moved on to adjust the next pigeon. My arms were shaky as I lifted myself back up. I thought I might faint. I faked my way through the rest of class with sweaty palms and a racing mind. I didn't even try to resist watching the clock. *Just let this be over already.*

In a haze, I walked out into the heavy Manhattan air in the same clothes I'd worn to yoga. I was eager to get out of class, for fear of what other unanticipated adjustments might occur. The street provided no refuge, as there were men everywhere. My eyes darted left to right as man after man crossed my path. I ran to my office around the corner. *What's happening to me?*

My coworker Megan walked into the kitchen as I was making tea.

"Uh, what are you doing?" she asked with a tone of urgency. Staring off into space, Dante on my mind, I'd been pulling the hot water lever down without a cup underneath. Megan grabbed a wad of paper towels and began to sop up the mess. I squatted down to help. She was no stranger to my clumsy ways, but she would never have guessed what was fueling them this time.

Megan and I had bonded instantly at our online advertising technology company. Neither of us knew what the hell we were doing, but we were both glad to be paid well to do it. We were artists, free spirits trapped in five-by-six cubicles. I'd replaced her as the bookkeeper when she was promoted to sales, and we shared nail polish remover, gum, and daily complaints. Megan vented about her on-again off-again office fling, Jared, and I lamented the monotony of billing. Nowadays, you just punch in the numbers and the software does it all for you.

Tucked away in my cubicle, I toggled between Quick-Books and People.com's "Hollywood's Sexiest Men." Pinned to the walls surrounding me were postcards for potlucks and art shows, and photos of my friends. All lesbians. I was haunted by their gazes as I explored my newfound man-lust. *What if I were truly attracted to men? Would I still have a place in my world? Could I betray the very people who cheered me on as Miss Lez?* I was reluctant to forfeit the rewards of coming out in the first place.

À la *Melrose Place,* the first girl I fell for was my college boyfriend's best friend. As a freshman, I passed much of my time in the student union, snacking and napping in between classes. One day, this guy boldly pushed my bag over and sat down next to me on the couch. We talked politics, debated, and then dated. Five months into our relationship, following an all-day student rights protest, he and his best friend, TJ, ended up at my house. TJ, with her black leather jacket, chain-smoking, and relentless sarcasm, was both alluring and crass. She was like no one I'd met before. As I tossed her a blanket to crash on my couch, I nearly tossed myself onto her.

I cuddled up next to my boyfriend, who was already snoring. My mind wandered into playback mode as I reflected on the many other times I'd felt a similar stirring inside. Stroking Stephanie's arm to lull her to sleep, hugging Karina goodbye when she moved to New Mexico, and dry humping my Mormon friend, Molly. Oh my God, I love girls! I fell asleep to the fantasy of a ride with TJ on her motorcycle. Too bad she had a girlfriend.

A few months later, my boyfriend and I broke up, and Karina came to visit. I hadn't seen her since she'd moved away, and I was smitten with her new bob haircut. It suited her. She'd always been more alternative than me and therefore seemingly open to things like kissing girls. She listened to bands like Patti Smith Group and The Wedding Present, and she usually wore only black. We passed the weekend roaming the streets of Northampton, eating ice cream and browsing thrift shops. On her last night, we got buzzed on bootleg beer at a party and raced each other back to my house. Giggling and out of breath, I said, "I've never kissed a girl, but if I had to pick one, it'd be you!" Then I dashed for my front porch.

"Does that mean I have to make the first move?" Karina yelled after me.

"Yep!" I ran up the stairs to my room, Karina close behind. And then we laughed, locked the door, and dove onto my bed, and she pinned me down and kissed me.

That first kiss led to others, with many other women. I became part of a tight-knit lesbian posse, and any short-lived relationships with men only further reinforced my interest in women. Upon graduation, I moved to San Francisco, where I fell madly in love with my first girlfriend, Amy. She was my bass teacher, but we only made it through two lessons, jumping way ahead of one finger per fret. Shortly after we began dating, I came out to my dad, knowing that Amy and I were more than a fling. The rest of my family had been easy. My mom and I are close, so she had known for years that I was dating women. And my brother was thrilled not to worry about his big sister at the mercy of potentially mean men. But I was nervous to tell my conservative Italian father and rehearsed for weeks in advance. Back in Connecticut, on a wintry November day, we went for a walk at aptly named Dike's Point, a park on the lake in our town. (And yes, it really is called that.) Halfway down the wooded path toward the shore, I abandoned all my well-planned scripts and heard myself blurt out, "Dad, I'm in love with my bass teacher, and her name is Amy!" My words echoed through the trees as I awaited his response. I tried to ignore my inner montage of horror stories of parents disowning their kids. And then he hugged me.

Early into our four-year relationship, Amy and I moved in together. We cooked, walked arm in arm to rent movies, and hiked Bernal Hill to bask in the Bay Area sun. It was 2001. The world was at war. But I finally felt at peace.

A few years later, moving to New York seemed like a natural migration. Amy and I both missed the East Coast, and several of our friends had moved there already. Soon after moving, we broke up harmoniously, needing space from each other to flourish in the next phases of our lives—she a focused musician; I a mess in the midst of my Saturn return. I had one other girlfriend after her and dated a handful of women here and there, but I otherwise kept busy exploring the city and hanging out with my family of friends. We had our bars, our parties, our picnics in the park, and our occasional trips upstate. Having built my whole world around women, the thought of dating men was absurd.

SCROLLING THROUGH THE pictures of celebrity men on my monitor, I was relieved to discover that they all looked the same, and I didn't find them all that attractive. That is, until I picked up right where I'd left off in high school, when I fell for the taut, just short of scrawny, skater and drug dealer types. Joseph Gordon-Levitt and Devendra Banhart. *Hmm. John Krasinski's kinda cute.* I googled my own secret male celebrity crush, Gael Garcia Bernal. He was hot in his gay sex scene in *Y Tu Mamá También.* Hey, a girl's gotta start somewhere. To take my mind off men, I actually did some work. I punched numbers into my Excel spreadsheet, relieved that no matter which way you turn them, two plus two equals four. But I still felt fidgety, so I strolled over to Megan's cubicle. She opened her desk drawer to hand me a mini Snickers. I popped it into my mouth, breaking the brand-new rule I'd set for myself of no sugar before noon.

"Meg, something weird happened this morning," I

confessed. She shut her eye shadow case to grant me her full attention. As I relayed the yoga teacher incident, my voice echoed across the canyon between who I was and what I was saying. I felt truly disoriented. My vision blurred, and the floor grew too soft to hold me. I gripped her desk for balance.

"So what should I do?" I asked Megan at the end of my story, exasperated and desperate for advice. She flailed her freshly manicured hands in my face, excited.

"Go to another class!"

# CHAPTER TWO

# I Want to Get Horizontal Like Yesterday

"What are you doing here?" I reprimanded in a harsh whisper.

The following week, my curiosity got the best of me and I bravely returned to yoga. I, too, raced to the room to place my mat up front, only to find that Megan had already reserved a spot for me: dead center. Dante walked up to the front of the room and stood directly across from me. He smiled hello and I blushed and nodded in return, such a serious student, so dedicated to my practice. I was so nervous, I'd stopped breathing, but luckily he was there to remind me.

"Inhaling, bring your arms into prayer position. Exhale into a forward bend, grounding the balls of your feet into the earth." Balls. *Ew.* I decided to focus on my practice like never before, perfecting my mating stance. Look at my right angle! I glanced around to check if Dante was looking. In downward dog, I stuck my butt out a little bit higher than usual. When it came time for pigeon pose I displayed my sloppiest rendition, but Dante was busy helping another woman across the room. I spent the entire class willing him to come over and touch me. Yoga was stressing me out.

At the end of class, Dante announced that his new book, *Peculiar Neutrality,* was available for sale. It was first come, first served, as he had only a few copies on hand. Back in the ladies' changing room, I hastily made my way to my locker, trying not to look like I was rushing. But we all were. Elbows were flying in the race to buy his book first. Designer dresses were crammed into bags without the usual care. Manolos flew through the air. I dove over a bench for my bag as two girls fought over a hair dryer. Now's my chance, I thought. Because I didn't mind my bird's nest of hair ('twas the season of bohemian chic), I was the first one out, or so I thought.

A few girls had skipped changing and were already in line. The girl that arrived after me hovered a little too close, so I turned around and cut her with my eyes, putting her back in her place: Behind Me. I bought his last two copies, claiming one was for my brother, and feigned interest in whatever it was about. We shared the elevator to the street and walked out together toward another studio, where he was to teach his next class. I took notice of the details in case I needed to stalk him someday. Tuesday. Eighteenth and Broadway. 8:41 a.m.. Our conversation carried us twelve blocks, along which I learned intimate things about him, like that he was spiritual but not religious, grew up in the suburbs, and preferred walking to riding the train. Just like me! I listened with the attentiveness of an anthropologist; Jane Goodall in jeans. In my mind's eye I was wearing glasses and taking notes. *An interesting specimen, indeed.* We talked about yoga and the sacred practice of being present in the body. I wanted him to put his present in mine. At his destination, he flashed me one of his big smiles and said goodbye. I nearly died.

At work Megan cornered me in the kitchen. "What happened? Tell me everything," she demanded, handing me a cup of tea—a sweet gesture, but she'd added sugar, which I never do. I sipped politely and flopped down on a stool.

"We walked out together," I said.

"You did?" She was one decibel short of yelling. The room seemed to ripple before me like a long stretch of highway on a steamy summer day.

"I don't know," I said wearily. "I think I'm just going to stop talking to him, ride it out for a bit."

"Ride him! Isn't that the point?" she said sternly, locking eyes with me before turning around to head for her desk. I shook my head and poured out my tea.

The following day, I spent the better part of the afternoon sorting through a slew of emails from confused clients because our company had implemented a new billing system that left everyone in the dark. I enjoyed fielding customer questions. It was the closest thing to helping people for a living since my six-month stint at counseling homeless youth. After half a year of staying up all night writing case studies and diffusing teenage temper tantrums, I'd left for a desk job at a nonprofit; still doing good, but on the safer, paper side. I'd later ended up in the corporate world when hit with the harsh reality of my student loan bills—loans I'd taken out to learn how to help people.

I nearly fell out of my ergonomic chair when I checked my personal email to find that Dante wanted to "be friends" on Facebook. That must mean he likes me! Facebook is much more personal than email! I perused his online photo albums; pictures from concerts, yoga retreats, Burning Man, and New Jersey, where he just had to live, as if being a man didn't make him foreign enough. I was leaning in close to my monitor to see if he was in fact wearing socks with sandals (a well-known lesbian trend) when the CEO startled me from behind.

"Who's that?" he asked.

I jumped and minimized the page, which made me look even guiltier.

"Oh, that's my brother's friend who asked him to deejay next week, but I'm not sure I can make it because I might go to Connecticut to see my mom, who just had knee surgery, and when I was five I stole a pack of gum from Woolworth's." I stopped to catch my breath. The CEO, a childhood friend and soon to be millionaire (our company was on the brink of being bought), was accustomed to my quirky ways. In middle school, I was curiously often "locked out of my house" and would walk up to his house to hang out. I was smitten, but he liked me "as a friend." In high school, when I grew into my buckteeth, the roles reversed. But when he finally came around, I turned him down and dated a skater boy dropout instead. This tells you a little something about my taste in men.

He dropped an invoice on my desk and turned to leave. My heart pounded as though I'd been caught cooking the books.

I returned to my in-box to find another eye-catching email, a request for an interview. *Velvetpark* magazine was doing a story on the pageant and wanted to hear from the new Miss Lez. What did I have to say for myself? Less than a month into my reign, I'd already shamed my people. My fantasies alone could have cost me the crown. Yet in a rainbow's myriad of ways, I couldn't have been gayer. I cat-sat, drank herbal tea, and in high school played field hockey. I'd been both vegan and vegetarian. I was a food co-op member. I drove a stick shift. As a kid I undressed Barbie and Skipper and made them kiss and touch boobs. I was even allergic to nuts.

I didn't want to want men. I didn't want to end up like those women I overheard in restaurants and bars, catching wind of phrases like "He always" and "He never," their martinis teetering on active fault lines. Many of my friends had nothing but horrible luck with men, and there was no reason to assume I'd be spared.

After work I waited for TJ at Cowgirl, a lesbian-owned diner famed for its hot sauce and hot clientele. Perusing the restaurant, I smiled inside at the sight of butches in jeans and tees, femmes in vintage dresses and the five-inch heels I could never walk in, gay men in tight tapered pants and pastel polo shirts tucked in just so, and everyone in between. Becoming who you are is no easy task, and I cherished my community of cowbois and grrrls. As a lover of women, I was one of them, a rebel by default. The thought of sacrificing that crushed me.

When TJ arrived, I caught myself eyeing her as a potential mate, flailing for an anchor to my land. I cocked my head to the side to see her from another angle, desperate to distract myself from thoughts of Dante, who posed in downward dog across my menu as I tried to choose a meal.

"What are you doing, jackass?" she asked when she caught me staring.

"Nothing. Did you cut your hair?"

ON THE TRAIN ride home, my book lay limply in my lap as I let my eyes wander over the crowd. Men were in suits, scrubs, basketball shorts, and jeans. They had short hair, shaggy hair, brown hair, gray hair; more hair on faces than heads since I'd last taken a look. They fiddled with their iPods and composed text messages to be sent later, from above ground. I wondered what they were writing and to whom. Perhaps they were planning the night with the rest of the guys, the time and place to gather to meet girls. Maybe they were no different from my friends and me.

Crossing over the bridge to Brooklyn, a lone star managed to shine brighter than the city. Gazing up, I wondered if it might be Venus. Then I wondered something else. Tomorrow I have yoga. *What will I wear?*

DANTE ADJUSTED ME twice during class the next day, which I credited to my new Lululemon pants. As I was rolling up my mat at the end, he handed me a postcard—an invitation to his birthday party, two weeks away. I smiled and set my hair free so that it fell down onto my shoulders from my yoga bun. *He wants me.* And then he passed the postcards out to the rest of the class.

I turned up the heat during the rest of the week, hoping for a date before his birthday. I didn't want to be yet another random girl lined up at his DJ booth vying for a chance to chat with him. I sent him a Facebook message, asking him about a performance artist he had mentioned during our walk. He wrote back almost instantly. I replied an hour later with a joke about the website he'd referred me to. He replied with a snarky remark. And we were off. Flirting with a guy seemed no different from flirting with a woman—not online at least.

Things seemed to be moving along at a satisfying pace over the course of the following week. We were emailing several times a day and had even begun to text. I was cracking up in my cubicle every half hour or so as he made fun of the pictures on my Facebook account. The flirtation factor was in full effect—until I received a blank email from him out of the blue. There was no subject. No text. Only an attachment: a photo of me in my Miss Lez tiara and sash. I panicked. I wasn't sure what to make of his email, so I attempted to make light of it in hopes the issue would float away.

"Oh, I forgot that my Miss Lez contract prohibits me from fraternizing with your kind."

He responded with a one-word email, one step up from the email with no text at all: "Goodbye."

I sank back in my chair, deflated, and didn't send a reply.

On the bus ride home from a work picnic later that week, sunburned and bloated from beer, Megan convinced me to text him, asserting, "You're a hot woman with a lesbian past. Trust me. No single straight man can resist that." I didn't quite trust her, but I sent a text anyway.

"I found a clause in my Miss Lez contract for professionals related to my well-being." I invited him to join us for drinks when he was done teaching his last class. Which I shouldn't have known was at seven forty-five on Spring Street.

An hour later, downing margaritas at an outdoor bar with Megan and her friends, after having declined an invite to meet up with TJ, I received a text back from Dante. "I want to get horizontal like yesterday." I squealed and passed my phone around the table for the straight girls' translation, unsure of his intention.

"Elena," Megan exclaimed. "Have you never heard that expression before? It means he wants to have *SEX* with you." She spelled out the word with her finger in the air.

I jumped up and down with excitement.

"Oh my God, what should I do?"

"Write back!" They all said in unison.

My hands were shaky as I typed my reply: "That's what I've been telling you all along."

"Telling me what?" he teased (or so I thought). My reply was bold, fueled by weeks of buildup and a generous amount of tequila.

"I'm in Union Square. Come here and I'll show you." I pressed "send" before I could really register what I'd written. For all the debilitating overthinking I'd done in my life, that would have been the time to employ it. A few minutes passed that felt like a lifetime. Why wasn't he responding? The girls all assured me he'd hopped on a train to meet me. My phone finally lit up and rang the bell tower ring tone, usually calming, suddenly a startling sound.

"I meant I'm exhausted and going to sleep."

I ducked under the table, trying to hide from myself and cursing out the girls as they consoled me.

"He's crazy. Who says that phrase and actually means sleep?"

"He's intimidated by your sexual past."

"He wants to wait to ask you on a real date."

"Maybe he smells bad from teaching all day."

And my personal favorite: "I've heard all yogis are celibate."

Excuses aside, there wasn't one single person at the table that did not find his message misleading. If the straight girls were confused, I was totally screwed (or not). I'd never understand men. I left, mortified, but secretly relieved, for it had occurred to me somewhere among messages that if he'd in fact shown up, I'd have had no clue what to do with him. I was on my way to throw my phone in the East River when it rang.

"Hello?"

"Hey baby-mama!" My childhood friend Keith makes Liberace look macho.

"Baby-daddy, oh thank God. I need you."

"Is it time?" At nineteen we'd made a pact that he would father my children should we both end up alone, gray, and gay. He was on his way.

"Not yet, love, but I'm getting there. What's up?"

"I'm in town for the night before I head to Florida for work. Come to Splash, bi-atch."

Perfect. Of all people, Keith would know how to deal with Dante. We'd been friends since we were ten, when my family descended upon his at an open house. My family bought the place, and his room became mine; the sky blue paint job replaced with pink flowered wallpaper, which he probably would have preferred. We played house now and then, though he never tried to kiss me like my other "husbands" at the time. In fact, I think he played the wife. Eternally single, as he was rarely in one place for more than a month, Keith ran a catering company that always teetered on the edge of chaos. I was constantly bailing him out, and it was time he returned the favor.

Upon arrival at Splash, Keith's friends fawned over me.

"She looks just like Sandra Bullock!"

"No, it's Ali MacGraw!"

They swung me around to the beat of "Borderline" blaring from the speakers. I could never resist Madonna, so I allowed myself to get swept up in the sweaty urgency of the club. Gay men loved that I was Miss Lez. They showed me off to their friends, parading me around like a doll. If I pursued my interest in men, would I be disappointing my gay boys, too? It was too loud to talk to Keith about men, so I soaked up their essence instead, studying the way they courted one another, staring each other down at the bar.

A couple of hours later, Keith and I stumbled out of the club and headed home to his apartment, where we curled up in bed and I broke the news. We stayed up all night having girl talk about boys. Keith couldn't have been more elated, finally able to put his years of experience to good use. Informed by a lifetime of disastrous one-night stands, he provided tuition on the art of hand jobs and rejection, and he assigned me a

MANtra: "Don't fall in love with the dick." He clarified, "A man and his penis are two separate things." *What did that even mean?* I felt more lost than I had the day before. Tucked in on his couch, the phrase hovered over me. *Don't fall in love with the dick. Don't fall in love with the dick.*

FRESH FROM A breakup with Jared again, Megan was depressed and in need of distraction. I was clearly in need of a complete overhaul when it came to relating to men, and I had to prepare for Dante's birthday party, which I was not yet deterred from attending. It takes more than humiliation to subdue me into submission, so Megan took me on as her protégé.

"First, we'll need to ensure your safety," she said, opening the door to the neighborhood sex shop, Toys in Babeland. I was nervous entering the store. At Babeland, one could purchase a penis, a magazine, and self-heating massage oil, all in one fell swoop. At one time I was quite comfortable walking in there. I'd greet the cashier, whom I most likely knew, and was usually given a discount.

Megan, however, led me straight to the condoms, the area along the wall with the books and DVDs, where the shy people tended to linger. Now I was one of them. With trepidation, I pointed to different condoms for her to put in a basket, opting for ones with a feminine twist—the purple Venus, the pink-packaged Birds-n-Bees, and for fun some

Tuxedos, to find out what that meant. I was shaking, guilt written all over my face, convinced that if any of my friends were to walk in, they'd see it.

"Oh come on!" Megan urged, a little too loudly.

"Oh my God, don't look," I said, putting my head down and shoving my hand into a condom bin to look busy.

"What?" Megan asked, turning around abruptly. "Lisa!" she yelled. Lisa was our coworker who everyone suspected was gay. She was married to a man but prone to conspicuous flirtations with the ladies (especially me). And there she was in the sex store with a woman, perusing the colorful array of insertables with names like Outlaw, G-Buddy, and Buck. Lisa's face turned red, like mine already was, as we greeted each other in the middle of the store, all of us empty-handed aside from Megan, who carried the basket of condoms. I laughed out loud. Laughing was the one thing that for some reason felt prohibited in Babeland. You could test out the bunny vibrators so they twirled around in your hand. You could try on harnesses in front of the mirror, but you were not supposed to laugh. To laugh would reveal thoughts of a sexually unhip woman—"Oh my God, you put that where?"

On our way back to Megan's house, we stopped every few blocks to gasp, "Can you believe we saw Lisa in there?" It wasn't too hard for me to believe, actually. There were plenty of people in closets of all kinds. I just never would have thought I'd be back in one.

From the bathroom at Megan's house, I heard the faint sound of moans and groans coming from a distant room. I assumed it was the neighbors. I opened her medicine cabinet, curious as to what I might find. An entire shelf was dedicated to scents. I had always thought a woman picked one perfume and wore it for the rest of her life, her signature scent, as I'd heard it referred to. But there on display were at least eight different bottles with names like Daisy, Elle, Blue Fields, and Woman. What does Woman smell like according to Calvin Klein? I sprayed it in the air and ran through it like my mom taught me to. I was a femme, but a hippie tomboyish one. I wore scented oils as perfume.

It turned out the moaning was coming from Megan's house. She had turned on a porn. I tiptoed toward the television, took a glance, and sat down with my hands covering my eyes.

"I don't think I'm ready for this," I said, queasy at the sight of male flesh. Megan pulled my hands away.

"It's time to learn some tips."

"Please don't use that word." Just then there was an extreme close-up of an extremely erect penis.

"What word? *Tip*? Do you prefer *cock*? *Head*? *Shaft*?" Megan teased. She was not about to let me off the hook, so I decided to sit back, open my eyes, and watch the woman on the screen perform the title of the film, *Hand-Job Extra,* the "extra" part being that she also used her feet. No wonder Megan was always running out for a pedi.

That night and several of the following, I found myself browsing straight porn sites on my computer at home. There was one couple in particular I became attached to. They were French, which somehow helped me shed some of my inherent puritanical inhibition. Watching them together turned me on. They seemed to truly be in love, and I was still a sucker for romance. I marked their page as a "favorite." I was proud of myself. I am a self-actualized woman! I can choose to have porn bookmarked on my computer if I want to! And then I removed it.

On the topic of removing things, it was time for my Brazilian, according to Guru Megan. Brazilian was short for Brazilian wax. I had gotten one a couple of years prior for the "I Heart Brooklyn Girls" calendar shoot, for which I had donned a *Baywatch* bathing suit—bright red and obscenely high cut. Megan dismissed that experience, explaining, "You may have had a Brazilian before, but you've never had "the Mariola." The place she sent me for my wax was so fancy that I had to be buzzed in, as if anyone in dire straits would rob a women's spa in Soho.

Apparently, Mariola was in high demand, because they had double booked her. I was squished in between two beautiful, well-dressed, entitled, disgruntled customers on a very small bench in the waiting room. I considered offering up my appointment as I recalled segments of Megan's description: "She gets every single last hair, using tweezers if she has to."

"Elena."

Legs sprawled, one foot wedged against the wall, I kept reminding myself that Mariola had seen it all.

"Hold here!" she ordered in her thick Polish accent. I was scared of her, so I obeyed, spreading my butt cheeks for her and cringing inside all the while. I did not recall feeling that exposed during my last wax job, or during any pap smear for that matter. I lay on my side. I lay on my stomach. I performed poses Dante could only dream of. I screamed with every strip. I tried to do some deep yogic breathing and focus on a visualization of birch trees blowing in the breeze, but I was panting like an overheated dog. And then it was done. And then she took out the tweezers.

Having conquered condom shopping, "the Mariola," and straight porn, Megan deemed me ready to go out and do some conquering of my own.

# CHAPTER THREE

# Before You Get on His Scooter, Be Sure He Knows How to Drive

A ny New Yorker will tell you, it's uncanny how often you bump into people you know in a city of eight million. It's bound to happen now and then, like when you're on the very street where they teach yoga. At the exact time they get out of class. So it wasn't my fault that I ran into Dante outside the health food store on his birthday.

In my defense, I had not slept a wink the night before, tossing and turning as I debated attending his birthday party. There is a famous quote, "Fear is born of fatigue and loneliness." So is insanity, I have found. Deliriously overtired and sexually charged, I was ready to combust, like a lit round shot stuck in a faulty cannon. According to my astrology guru, Susan Miller, as a Leo, Dante was allegedly pioneering and impulsive—the perfect match for Miss Lez. Perhaps he just needed to be taken by surprise.

I recognized him from half a block away. There was no mistaking his gait. The slight bounce in his step, the gym pants, and the clincher, his yoga mat. He was unwrapping a protein bar, the snack of choice for a yoga teacher on the run.

"Dante!" He didn't hear me.

"Dante!" I picked up my pace. So did he. At that point in my position, a sane person would have stopped, turned around, and walked away. Me? I chased him.

The metal buckles on my backpack unfastened and started banging against the bottles of goddess salad dressing in my grocery bag. With my unzipped jacket whipping in the wind and my hair still wet from the morning's shower, I must have looked as crazy as I felt.

As I closed in on him, I noticed the white wires of headphones bobbing against his shoulders as he trotted toward the stoplight. To my surprise, and even more so to his, I watched myself as if I were in a slow-motion movie scene: I grabbed ahold of his backpack. And tugged. He turned around with the most horrified expression, assuming, as any city dweller would, that he was being mugged. He didn't seem relieved to discover it was me.

"I wasn't stalking you, I swear," I said defensively, out of breath. "I decided to get a kombucha." As soon as the words came out of my mouth, I wanted to dive into the nearest manhole and crawl my way back to Brooklyn. I felt like Baby in *Dirty Dancing,* swallowing her first words to

Patrick Swayze, "I carried a watermelon." However, unlike watermelon, a sexy, refreshing summer treat, kombucha is a fermented mushroom tea. It is not pretty. Picture a translucent glass jar filled with urine-colored juice in which hazy clouds of mold float through stalactites of more mold. And then imagine someone threw up in it. Kombucha stakes claim to healing ingredients, such as naturally occurring probiotics, which are good when you have a yeast infection. Or diarrhea.

Dante hadn't said a word but rather just stood there silent and stunned. I didn't know how to redeem the situation, so I said the first thing that came to mind.

"Happy Birthday!"

"Thanks."

The light changed and he crossed the street. I crossed my heart to give up on men forever and ever, amen, and went home to google new yoga studios.

I did manage to resist attending his birthday party, but my vow turned out to be like giving up drinking in the midst of a horrible hangover: "Dear God, if you make me stop puking, I'll never drink again." The Dante detox lasted a whole of two weeks, until a mutual friend's dinner party e-vite displayed his RSVP as "attending." With one last chance at winning him over, or at the very least redeeming a tidbit of my dignity, I dressed up for the big night. I slipped into a loose black satin blouse with a peephole to my cleavage, skinny jeans so tight

I had to lie down to get into them, and the "starter heels" Megan had lent me, insisting men prefer them to flats.

I was nervous ringing the doorbell.

"Elena?" My brother, also a friend of the host, eyed my outfit curiously, accustomed to my flouncy gypsy tops, leggings, and boots. I hobbled into the apartment after him. The shoes that were mildly uncomfortable when I'd first put them on by then felt like walking in ice skates.

I grabbed a glass of wine and sat down to catch him up. There was no way out of it. We were not only siblings but also neighbors and good friends. Our worlds were too intertwined for me to try to hide from him. I confessed that I'd dressed up for a guy. He was taken aback, having been grateful for a lesbian sister. When I shared with him my sudden rekindling of interest, he subtly tried to deter me. Though he's younger, my brother is prone to better decision-making, having been granted a more generous portion of judgment genes. I probably should have listened.

The first hour of the party dragged on. I sipped wine and willed Dante to arrive. He didn't. I sipped more.

As the night unfolded, I found myself flirting with the other guys there, practicing for the real thing. My poor brother steered clear of me, not fond of the new Elena. He was accustomed to the version with little tolerance for men. But I was finding it surprisingly easy to laugh at their dumb jokes.

"Why yes, you're right, the BlackBerry scroll ball is like

a little clit!" It was relatively painless to play along when I wanted something in return. And as it turned out, it wasn't just Dante I wanted. I was on a man mission. My curiosity had been piqued, and I had to put Megan's lessons to use, not to mention my hard-earned money. A Brazilian wax with Mariola is not cheap.

Three hours into the night, uninspired by the selection of single straight men on the party menu, I poked around the hors d'oeuvres and snagged the last piece of cake.

"You didn't," said a voice from above. A sharply dressed man hovered over me as I swallowed the second half of the slice.

"I did." I washed down the last of the cake with the last of my wine. "Where did you swoop down from?"

"I just got off work," he said, reaching across the table too close to me and dutifully refilling my glass with shiraz. He was careful not to spill any on his crisp white shirt, which he'd unbuttoned at the top. Though I knew nothing about ties, a nice-looking one hung loosely from his neck. His sandy brown hair was mussed in just the right way; naturally, after a long day's work, as opposed to crafted with some overpriced pasty product with a name like Morning After. He had a little bit of the Joseph Gordon-Levitt baby-face thing going on. I wondered if he wished he looked older.

"What do you do that you get off at midnight?" I asked, nearly losing my balance. The sugar rush had set in.

"I'm a lawyer, a first year, which means I'm basically their bitch. I stay until my bosses leave and often much later."

That was the point where my brother left the party, only after unsuccessfully urging me to pass up the lawyer for late-night sibling sundaes. He'd tried his best. But if ice cream couldn't stop me, nothing could. I hugged my brother goodbye, sending him off with the same famous last words I'd been saying his whole life: "Don't worry!"

The lawyer invited me to join him on the couch, where he promptly picked up my feet and started massaging them. After walking in those shoes, I was putty in his hands. It was a little embarrassing, flirting with him in front of everyone at the party. But I wasn't bothered enough to stop him, which is one of the great things about getting older. You care less and less what people think. When the party started to thin out, I excused myself to the bathroom.

*Elena, you can do this.* I fixed my hair in the mirror. *You've come this far.* I was anxious, assuming I would have to take some initiative if I were to go home with the lawyer. With the women I'd been after in the past, I'd often offered the first signal of interest. There is nothing worse than hitting on a girl and having her say, "Sorry, I'm straight." Since I was femme, I liked to help erase any ounce of doubt, for there is a complex dance performed at lesbian bars. Is she gay? Is she here with a guy? Is she here with her gay friends? Does she have a girl-friend? Has she dated my best friend?

When I found the lawyer back in the living room, he was wearing his coat and holding mine. I guess the dance for straight people is more like the two-step. One, "You're single?" Two, "Me too."

"Looks like the party's over," he said, holding my coat open behind me to slip into. "I live right down the street. We can get my scooter and I can give you a ride home if you'd like. I just got it." I smiled to myself, sliding my arms into the ripped lining of my sleeves.

It's hardly necessary to say that we ended up in his living room, on his couch, for yet another foot massage. Outside his apartment door, he'd invited me in. Once inside, he'd offered me a drink. Each question provided an opportunity for me to turn back, but something inside compelled me to say, "Yes, yes, and yes." His apartment was sparsely decorated in a stark, minimalist style. The walls were painted cloudy sky gray and were bare but for a giant psychedelic poster of Buddha. The kitchen was open to the living room, separated by a full island bar, bachelor-pad style. I couldn't help comparing his kitchen to my ex, Amy's. When we'd first met, I'd felt right at home at her place, scattered with tea lights, plants, and incense sticks, her cat Kiki roaming around. In comparison, the lawyer's place might as well have been Mars.

I sat myself down on a bar stool and watched him pour two drinks. I giggled, giddy from rebelling against my customarily prudish disposition, my lesbian identity, and my brother.

"What's funny?" he asked, wielding the cocktail shaker like a pro.

"How long have you lived here?" I asked, swiveling around on the stool and changing the subject. I felt like a teenager again, like we were stealing gin from his parents' liquor cabinet for a party we shouldn't be having.

"A few years," he answered, leading me into the living room. It was the dawn of fall, during a week that felt more like winter, so he threw a couple of logs on some kindling. We had a fire going in no time.

He grabbed my foot again and picked up where we'd left off at the party. Then he leaned over to kiss me. I closed my eyes and moved toward him. His face felt scratchy, like an old frayed toothbrush. I realized I'd been spoiled by women's silken flesh. Even so, there turned out to be an abundant amount of chemistry between us as we made out in front of the fireplace. It was hot. When he went to touch my boob, I stopped abruptly and sat up.

"I want to take it slow because it's been years," I said. "I haven't been with a man in many years. But I haven't been alone either. I've been with women, and I'm not sure I'll remember what to do." And before he had a chance to respond, I tackled him. I jumped right up on top of him and slid his shirt over his head in one swift motion, impressing myself. We made our way up to his room, and as he pulled my shirt up, I tried to get out of my skinny jeans, twisting and turning to peel them off.

When I went to lie down on the bed, he stopped me and placed a condom in the palm of my hand. I hadn't practiced that part with Megan. I tossed it back at him.

"I want to watch you put it on." I fell onto the bed in what I hoped was a flirtatious fashion.

And then we were having sex. And it felt good, and it was fun, and it was true what Megan had said: It was just like riding a bike. But his bike didn't feel all that different from those of the women I'd been with—combine the right material with the right rhythm, and a dildo does the trick just as well. Sorry boys. We navigated each other like any two strangers would, trying this way and that, standing up, lying down, sitting up, spin me round. Sex is sex is sex. What was different from being with a woman was how he acted afterward. He pulled back the covers and we crawled underneath. Starry eyed, I shifted over to his side of the bed and flung my arm across his chest. He grunted, moved my hair out of the way, and rolled over to face the opposite wall. Me Man. Man No Cuddle.

The next morning he woke me very early for a Saturday. He had to leave for work and offered to buy me brunch beforehand.

"We can take my scooter," he said, beaming with pride. We headed outside into the brisk, bright morning. He was still cute in the glare of sober daylight. *Phew.*

"Wait here," he said, jogging around the corner of the

building. I heard the sound of a motor revving. He returned on his shiny new Vespa, approaching me very slowly, wobbling like Bambi on ice. I could tell he didn't know how to drive it, but in the tradition of poor discernment, I hopped on the back and strapped on my helmet. I grew up riding on Vespas in Italy. I knew what it felt like to ride with my cousin Marco, a seasoned driver, at the helm, and riding with the lawyer was not it. Just when I was about to suggest he drop me off at the nearest subway station, we hit a patch of wet leaves and crashed. The bike slid out from under us and landed on my leg, burning a hole right through my pants and through my skin as well. I screamed. He strained to pull the scooter up off me, and I hopped to the sidewalk to inspect my leg. The muffler had burned his first initial into my calf. The lesbian gods were angry.

"It's just the first layer of skin," he consoled.

You would think getting burned on my first date with a man would have scared me off, but I am a very stubborn person with a high threshold for pain. Besides, when I told Megan about it, she didn't seem adequately phased.

"But he was kind of a jerk about it." I said, trying to get her to understand.

"Elena," she put her hand on my shoulder and gave me a look of condolence. "If you want to go out with men, you have to lower your expectations."

"That might be the worst advice I've ever heard."

THE LAWYER AND I had been dating for a couple of weeks when he invited me upstate for the weekend. I accepted the offer, hiding my excitement. I took it as a turning point. Until then, there wasn't much opportunity to talk, having spent most of our time in bed on the few nights he left the office before midnight. It was lights out and clothes off. And in the morning we took the subway together during rush hour; hardly the chance to chat. I was looking forward to us getting to know one another.

On the train to Hudson, I made little comments here and there about the pretty scenery passing by the train window, but he didn't take the bait. Instead, he nodded and continued reading the *Wall Street Journal* and sipping his coffee in silence. Accustomed to the chatter of women, I fidgeted in my seat in discomfort. I searched my bag, not looking for anything in particular except perhaps some understanding of the foreign species seated next to me. I'd always heard, "Men don't talk," but was it meant that literally? I noticed my squirming bothered him, so I did it more.

His friends greeted us at the train station in their Toyota Prius. They were a cool couple, a graphic designer and an environmental engineer, hence the hybrid car. The lawyer suddenly appeared to have plenty to say, updating his friends on his work woes and recent obscure music discoveries. We headed to their house and dropped off our bags. They were staying down the street with some friends in order to give us the place to ourselves. We freshened up and joined them for a feast of Mexican food.

"My friends and I made tamales from scratch the other day," I said, reaching for more salsa, surprised to feel so nervous around new people. "They really take forever. My friend grew up making them with her m—"

"*Th-am-alez.* That's how you say it. I had the best *th-am-alez* in *Co-lombia,*" the lawyer interrupted, annunciating dramatically. I sat with my mouth gaping open, the last words of my sentence suspended in midair. It was the first of what would turn out to be many interruptions that weekend as he and his friends talked about Noam Chomsky and meditation and art. For the lack of talking the lawyer did on the train, he made up for it with his friends. I felt small and stupid and unseen. It had been awhile since I'd felt so insecure. I recalled feeling that way when I was younger, around guys I wanted to impress, walking on eggshells, trying to say the right savvy, intelligent thing. I wasn't that malleable girl anymore but rather a confident, self-assured woman. But I had grown accustomed to the company of women, with whom I generally felt included and heard.

We went for a hike, at which point I gave up entirely, walking alongside them without saying a word. Instead I took in the landscape, the river and trees that saw me. It was jarring how seamlessly I could resort to that dark silent place inside, like it had been awaiting my return all along. By evening I was on the verge of tears.

The house we were staying in had grown cold, the sun no longer casting streams of light across the floor. So we ended up right back where we'd started: in front of another fire. Only it wasn't so hot. We sat in silence for a while, and I wanted more than anything to go home. The lawyer eventually placed another log on the pile and to my surprise scooped me onto his lap.

"I'm sorry if I've been cold with you," he said, "but I'm taking it slow because I'm not sure where I want this to go." He fiddled with the fire poker. The log he had just put on was too long for him to close the glass fireplace door. We were sitting in front of an open flame. He grabbed the burning log with the fire prod and shoved it to the back of the pile. Sparks flew, and I knew instantly it was my split ends that had been singed, because the smell of burned hair is unmistakable. The too-big log balanced precariously on top of the ashes of the wood we'd already burned. He jammed the door a few times, and just as I was about to interject and suggest that brute force might not be the best approach, the door shattered into a thousand shards of glass.

I had to hold back laughter, because in the little time I'd known him, one thing was crystal clear. He hated looking like a fool. *Maybe all men do?*

"Go to bed," he offered. "I'll clean this up and wait for the fire to burn down." On my way out of the room, I tossed him a pillow to sit on while he waited. I was trying my best to be nice. But it missed his lap and bounced off his face, sending his glasses into the pile of ash. It was impossible to hold back laughter after that. I erupted into hysterics, finally releasing all the tension that had been building since we boarded the train. He didn't laugh along.

"I'm sorry," I said, in between cackles.

"Just try to be a little more careful next time," he replied condescendingly, retrieving his glasses and wiping off the lenses with his shirt. I felt like a kid being reprimanded. His tone sent me into even stronger muffled convulsions, so I ran into the bedroom and let the laughter loose into my pillow. And then I passed out happily, alone.

In the morning the tension was palpable. We said goodbye to his friends and offered to pay for the broken door. I was dreading the talk we would inevitably have on the train, the one where we'd discuss our differences and decide to go our separate ways. But I was still thinking in girl mode, where, you know, you communicate. Upon boarding the train, he affectionately adjusted the tag on my shirt, rested his head on my shoulder, and drifted off to sleep. I was baffled. *Did he really not realize something was terribly wrong between us?* It dawned on me that having sex with guys and relating to them are two very different things. At Grand Central, I pulled him aside at the subway entrance.

"Thank you so much for this weekend, but I think we are too different to continue to . . . " And then the tears came.

I attempted to explain how I felt, but I was too emotional to form the words.

"You barely talked to me. I felt invisible. I just want to go home," I said.

He was dumbfounded and pulled me toward him.

"I'm sorry. I didn't realize you were having a bad time."

"That's the point," I said in between sobs. "You didn't even notice. It's like you're in your own world." And for a split second he softened.

"You're not the first person to say that to me."

And then he stepped away from me and said, "Well, I would have liked to spend some more time together, but I didn't think you were the girl I was going to marry or anything." He looked down and smoothed out the wrinkles on his shirt.

I laughed and shook my head, feeling like myself again, back on my New York turf. Then I turned to head toward the Q train, which I'd grown to count on to take me home.

# CHAPTER FOUR

# Early Detection Testing

I wasn't late and I'd always used protection with the lawyer, but it had been a while since a penis had come within three feet of me. I was paranoid. When I darted into my neighborhood pharmacy for a pregnancy test, I felt like I was back at Babeland, overridden with guilt and acting shifty, as if I were planning to shoplift. Of course, I found myself face to face with a lesbian couple I knew, in the middle of the magazine aisle. Thankfully, at that moment I had been innocently browsing *Us Weekly,* stalling my purchase. Even so, my cheeks flushed to match the pink boxes that sat on a shelf two aisles over. I'd walked by the pregnancy tests three times already, conjuring up the courage to grab one and bring it up to the cashier. They lived right next to the UTI medicine, for which I'd limped into the same store the month before.

If you've ever had a UTI, you know what the initials

stand for—urinary tract infection—and you also know that you have to run to the bathroom every five minutes for a phantom pee. When you finally do collapse onto the toilet seat, it feels like you're pushing out trickles of battery acid, accompanied by muffled howls of disbelief: "Oh My God, Oh My God, Oh My God." I'd had UTIs in the distant past, when I'd dated guys before. They are usually the result of too much friction (not enough lube), dehydration, or stress. If you feel one coming on, you can often chase it off with cranberry juice and vitamin C. But that one had come out of the blue.

It started with the twinge of a vaguely familiar feeling, down there. I couldn't nip it in the bud, and I couldn't help but take it as a sign that I shouldn't be sleeping with men. I nearly crawled over to the Duane Reade drugstore across from my house and purchased God's Greatest Invention: those little orange pills that turn your pee a numb neon orange. They were prescription only back when I'd last needed them in the early nineties, so the triumph of finding them over the counter, next to the Monistat, rivaled the time I stumbled upon a six-foot-tall Swatch watch on a family trip to Switzerland. With that hanging on my bedroom wall, I was the coolest girl at school. For a week.

"We haven't seen you around in awhile," said one of my friends. "What have you been up to?" I hugged each of them in their lofty retro down vests, a sure sign that fall was under way. Where had I been, they wanted to know? I honestly couldn't say.

"Oh, I've been working a ton. Start-ups," I said, nodding my head as if in agreement with them. I overzealously petted their newly adopted, blind, three-legged dog while they eyed me inquisitively. I'd never been known to stay at work a minute past six, which was one hour past the time I would have liked to leave. Many of my coworkers would stay until eight or nine, but they were the computer programmers and salespeople. As the bookkeeper, I kept banking hours (I'd decided). And since no one had ever protested, that's the way it was. Besides, I was the eccentric artist at work, so other rules applied to me. Like, I was allowed to take up half the kitchen counter for my rice cooker and stink up the office with steamed broccoli. So when I had to run to the bathroom to pee every twenty minutes on the first day of my UTI, no one batted an eye. They probably assumed I was on the Master Cleanse again.

"Who's this?" I asked, picking up their ragged, milky-eyed Chihuahua.

"That's Chico," they replied in unison, beaming. "We rescued him from a kill shelter. Hey, you should come over for wine tonight. We redid the kitchen."

"Yeah, we did it all ourselves," my other friend chimed in. "Rented a power sander and everything."

I would have liked going over to their house to hang out. But I was nervous. They'd be sure to ask probing questions, and I'd never been good at lying. My mom always said, almost pitying me, "Oh, Elena, you can't get away with anything." From hoarding the forbidden Garbage Pail Kids cards to skipping out on assembly at school, I always got caught. And although something huge had shifted, some things never change.

I left the drugstore with only a magazine. At home I sat down at my table for four and browsed an empty article about the feud between Jennifer Aniston and Angelina Jolie. For the first time in a while, I felt alone. The loneliness was accompanied by a wave of nausea, which reinforced my pregnancy fear. To stave off the panic, I searched online for common symptoms:

- Nausea, check.
- Swollen or tender breasts, check.
- Fatigue, check.
- Unusual food cravings, check.

Falling farther into the chasm, I clicked on a link for a due-date calculator. Based on my last period, my maybe baby would be a Gemini. *Nooo!* I called TJ.

"Dumbass, I thought you were dead," she said, sounding extra husky.

"Don't get your hopes up. Let's go get some tea."

"Tea? Make it Bloody Marys. I think I'm still drunk from the Cock Block Party last night. Hey, where were you? Brianna was deejaying. I was sure you'd be up on stage putting on your S&M show." I cringed. One benefit of not going out to lesbian parties was that I was drinking less. Knowing all the bartenders on a personal basis always (and usually unfortunately) meant free unlimited drinks. The last time I'd gone out, my friend Brianna and I were chatting (yelling, rather) over the deafening music during our long wait for the ladies' room. I blame whiskey and the charged atmosphere for the incident that followed. When Brianna enthusiastically told me she'd recently seen Madonna in concert, I screamed, "No way!" and slapped her square across the face. To this day I have no idea why, and I have not had any more whiskey. I apologized profusely and excused myself to the pizza place up the street, where I soaked up the alcohol with a slice of cheese twice the size of my head.

"I told you never to remind me of that, asswhole." (This was how TJ both pronounced and spelled it, so I did too, for I was not about to correct her.) She also thought Stonehenge was Stone Hedge, as I discovered on a cross-country trip we made together once. She was sure she was right, arguing that it made more linguistic sense, the site being somewhat of a hedge and all. When I won the bet, she was the one pumping gas for the rest of the three-thousand-mile trip—sun, rain, or snow, all three often appearing within the same state.

"Listen," I said, in between sips of my virgin Bloody Mary (with extra pickles, please), "I have to tell you something. I've barely told a soul, and I want to keep it that way."

"Well, you can tell me. I have no soul," TJ said, trying to spear an olive with her straw. I could always count on TJ. She listened attentively as I confessed my yoga teacher obsession and then, the graver felony, sleeping with the lawyer and my potential pregnancy predicament.

"Wow," TJ said, sitting back in her chair, disturbingly pleased with herself. "If I've ever wanted blackmail material, this trumps anything I could have thought up on my own, Miss Lez."

"Trump? That's a big word for you.""

"I think I heard it on TV yesterday. Anyway, when were you, you know?" TJ tilted her head as if this were supposed to imply what she was asking, but I wasn't catching on.

"When was I what? Doing it?"

"Duh, jackass, yes, but when you were doing it, where were you—"

"Oh, his house, my house, this one time almost at his office, but then he met me at a bar instead, and from there we—"

"Ack! TMI! No, idiot, when were you, ugh, I can't believe you're making me say it. Where were you in your *cy-cle*?"

I let out one of my famous guffaws, turning the heads of the other patrons.

"I hate you," TJ said, and got up to head to the men's restroom.

I motioned for the waiter and ordered a piece of the Brooklyn Blackout cake I'd seen on my way in.

"And two forks, please."

The blackout kicked in back at my house, where TJ and I lay comatose on the couch, her feet on my lap, me refusing to massage them.

"Stupid, you're not pregnant. Just go get a goddam test and get it over with. Remember when you just knew you had Lyme disease because you were tired all the time, but it turned out you're just lazy?"

"Are you insane? I can't go back in there."

"Do you want me to go get the fucking thing for you?"

"You would do that for me?"

"No, jackass, not to save your life. Mine, maybe. But not yours."

"Thanks."

"Now tell me. What exactly brought this whole thing on? Are you bored with women? You wanna have a baby? A lot of chicks suddenly decide they want a baby the 'easy way' and end up with a dude. Usually happens around age thirty or so. If that's the case, you're past due. Tick tock, tick tock."

"No, no, that's not it."

"Then what? You miss the 'real thing'? Come on, just tell me. Every butch on the planet wants to know if we're second rate."

"Honestly, that's not it at all, and for the record, the 'real thing' is overrated."

"I like that answer."

"The thing is, I don't know, but I do know you won't be the only person to ask me. It's the questions I dread the most. If other people find out about this, I'm in no place to give answers. God knows, I'm asking myself the same thing every day."

"Alright. Well I think you're insane, and I strongly advise against it, but if for whatever reason you insist upon chasing down guys, then you're going to have to toughen up. If they're anything like me, they're dogs."

"I've already discovered that, thank you very much. I definitely don't want a relationship with a guy. I just kind of want to experiment some more."

"Oh. Well if it's just sex you're after, that should simplify things. You just have to get your heart out of the way."

"And how exactly do I do that, Tin Man? Press eject and place it on my nightstand for safekeeping?"

"It's more like control-alt-delete. Have you not been observing me all this time?"

"In fact, I have, which is why we're not together."

"Exactly. Now listen carefully, because it's complicated and can't always be taught. Ready? My top-secret recipe for dating survival is: Just Don't Care. I can say it slower. Just. Don't. Care. Do you understand?"

"Not really," I said, shifting in my seat, recalling when I was in love with TJ many years prior and how I'd pursued her in vain.

"If you find yourself starting to feel anything—anything at all—stop. Walk out. Put your boots on and run. Don't return calls. Sleep with someone else. Go for a drink. Knit if you have to . . . but just don't care."

"I don't knit."

"It doesn't mean you gotta be a raging asshole. You can have fun. That's what it's about. But you just got to keep your guard up. Got it, lesbo? You need them to know up front that they cannot count on you, that you are inconsistent, selfish, untrustworthy, and a whole lot of fun. Are you up for this?"

"Honestly, I don't think so. It sounds like a lot is involved to stay uninvolved," I replied, weary of TJ's strategy.

"There are tricks to it. For instance, keep vampire hours. Don't ever see them in the daylight. No long walks, no meeting their friends, don't take out your freaking photo albums and go through your life history. All you do is send a text, tell them to meet you at a bar, and that's it. It's actually quite simple. Don't give me that look. I know I'm not a good person. And neither are you. You hide it better, but I can see right through your little hippie save-the-whales routine. You make them tea and tabbouleh, and you get away with your satanic hypoglycemic episodes. You're halfway there already. If you want to survive this little experiment you got going, you need to listen to me. I suggest you start by putting your heart in one of your annoying little herb jars you got on your windowsill; yeah, the ones right next to your prayer stones and Joni Mitchell albums. Now, ready to give it a shot?"

"Totally," I said, and put the kettle on for some tea.

WHOLE FOODS WAS always packed unless you got there at the precise moment they opened. The long lines provided for way too much time to peruse the impulse items: Beekman Boys goat milk soap, Luna Bars, vitamins, and the most high-risk of temptations, the magazines. In spite of myself, I reached past my usual reads, *O, Dwell,* and *Bust: For Women with Something to Get Off Their Chests,* and opted instead for *Fit Yoga* (For Women Suddenly Wanting to Get Off with Their Yoga Teacher). The cover was graced by another Elena, a famous yoga instructor, for whom students formed a line around the block. I bet Dante would have overlooked the whole lesbian thing for *that* Elena. With her expertise in heart-opening anusara, I doubted she was chasing people down the street. Did she feel fully centered and whole all the time? I opened to the table of contents. How could I feel grounded, too?

Perhaps the answer was in the feature article, "Grow Your Love." Better yet, maybe it was tucked away in the very bottom right corner, in a little sea-foam-green box: "The Dante Earthdance Playlist." Before I could get a glance at the track titles, it was my turn in line. I tossed the magazine into my basket, careful not to crush my organic lavender dark chocolate bars (plural).

On the walk back to the office, I was nearly plowed over by a hoard of tourists in Union Square. I retrieved my new magazine from my bag. Maybe I had been brainwashed during yoga class by all those songs Dante played at the barely audible level. Who knows what messages they were sending? However, according to his list of favorites, the messages followed a consistent theme: mother earth, embrace the divine, goddess bless. If anything, a playlist like that should turn a straight girl gay.

At work, I spent the afternoon formulating the first of many theories I would come to mull over. I was six years old the summer I learned to swim. My parents had shipped me off to Italy to spend some time with my relatives. A summer when you're six feels like a lifetime. My first time flying alone, the way my independence surged inside, I must have grown two inches along my stroll through the gate. I was big. Little did I know, there were six pairs of eyes on me, not to mention my own personally assigned flight attendant. She hung a giant name tag around my neck and handed me a book of stickers. They came with a foldout scene of a blank landscape, laminated so that I had a plethora of options for the placement of the various images: animals, people, cars, planes, clouds. I could place a person here and a tree there and then move the person to sit on top of the tree. If I wanted it to, a cow could swim in the sea. We flew over New York City, the whitecapped Atlantic Ocean, farmland reminiscent of jigsaw puzzles, and finally the Swiss Alps. For all I knew from my window seat and sticker set, the world was vast and malleable.

Being half Italian, I'd grown up knowing there was always an alternate way of doing things, and at the very least, two ways of describing them. That summer I learned I could wade my way through the shallow end or, as my cousin Marco taught me, dive into the deep end of *la piscina* and swim. It's a blessing and a curse, a mind that's wide open. It seems I've tried to live ten lifetimes in one. From my first career choice of gift wrapper after a Christmas shopping trip to Sears with my mom, to photographer, to marine biologist, the list is endless. That last one actually almost stuck when I started my freshman year of college in the School of Fisheries Science. But by my second semester I had switched to women's studies, impassioned by an imaginary scenario my professor threw out for the class to debate: "If a black man and a white woman were running for president, who would win?" The conversation was heated and I grieved the fact that I'd never see such a thing in my lifetime. Fifteen years later, that question is no longer hypothetical. That's the thing about change. It happens.

"But what are you going to do with that degree when you graduate?" My father's voice still echoes from across the dinner table as if it were yesterday.

*Why, Papa, clearly I'm going to spend my days pondering the meaning of life from my navy blue bookkeeping cubicle.* I was drawn to office jobs like a dog to its kennel, a seat belt for my short attention span. Within the seven years I'd worked in New York, I had made business plans for a wine bar, an ice cream parlor, and a cheese shop. I'd pondered the Peace Corps, completed one term toward an art therapy license, inquired into massage therapy training, and researched beauty schools (hairdressing my long-standing go to). Was my unexpected interest in men yet another symptom of my restlessness, my innate compulsion to consider absolutely every option life has to offer?

IN THE END, I opted for the generic drugstore pregnancy test, though Megan tried to steer me toward a digital one. I just couldn't fathom spending $16 when I could expect the same (hopefully negative) result from one that cost $10.99. I would spend the difference on a celebratory ice cream cone.

"Just get me whichever one's cheapest," I'd said, handing her a twenty. When Megan returned with the test, she dropped it onto my desk, double bagged—a thoughtful gesture on the part of the female cashier, who also double bagged our tampons.

I read the instructions five times by the dim light of the ladies' room stall. One line means not pregnant; two means I'm doomed. Okay, okay. After I peed my five-second stream, all there was left to do was wait. At three minutes, I could check the test, but of course I sat there watching it. The second pink line seemed to appear before my eyes, but every time I blinked, it returned to the ghostly possibility of a line it had been at the start. *Tick tock, tick tock.* At the end of three minutes, there was still one sole line, but a heightened awareness had been conceived: *I am playing with fire.*

# CHAPTER FIVE

# The L Word

Having successfully avoided Williamsburg for the bulk of my time in New York, I gave in to an invitation to a friend's birthday party, with the ulterior motive of meeting men. Though it's located in my borough, getting to and from Williamsburg involves taking the subway from Brooklyn into Manhattan and then back into Brooklyn. I'll be kicking myself someday, when someone other than me makes millions off a shuttle business between the two hipster destinations, Ditmas and The Burg.

From the few times I'd subjected myself to one, there were certain things I had come to expect from a party in Williamsburg. There would be eccentric music pumped through an expensive sound system—songs by artists I had never heard of but that everyone else claimed to know. The loft would be covered in art I didn't understand, like lightbulbs piled up in a corner. And there would be lots of guys clad in thick-rimmed oversize glasses, tapered jeans, and turquoise nylon Windbreakers two sizes too small. A few times early in the evening, one of them would come over to me and seem to be flirting, only there would be no smiling or laughing involved, because hipsters don't express emotion, so it was a little hard to tell.

"Do you work at The Wilderness with Ben?" The question was aimed at me by a smug-looking guy as he nonchalantly popped the top off his Chimay. He didn't offer me one from his personal stash.

"No," I answered. "We went to school together."

"Oh, where did you guys go to school?"

"UMASS Amherst," I answered, prepared for the follow-up sigh of disappointment that I was accustomed to in a crowd like that. An air of judgment hung around the room. Whenever I'm around insecure people, I start to feel uncomfortable myself, like my arms are no longer attached to my body. In my head I concocted a defense: *I chose UMASS—it wasn't my safety school. I'm not even from Massachusetts.* But that would only make me sound as self-conscious as I felt, so I kept the thoughts to myself and instead sipped my PBR and drifted off to a daydream.

I'd been accepted to the University of Rhode Island, into the Department of Marine Biology. Having known since junior year that I'd end up at URI, I paid little attention to the surroundings as my mom drove me in her maroon Isuzu Trooper to check out my future school. We parked the car and grabbed some lunch before beginning the campus tour. An even bigger fan of dessert than I am, my mom ordered a piece of chocolate cake for us to share.

"This is orgasmic!" I gasped, the molten cake melting in my mouth. I was seventeen. My mom spit out her coffee. She'd never heard me say the word *orgasm* before. In fact, I'd never said it before then, let alone had one. But I was checking out a college. I was almost an adult.

The tour left me feeling unsettled. The campus was beautiful and the people were nice, but URI just didn't feel right. Although for two years I'd been set on going there, I said, "Let's check out UMASS, too." Part of becoming an adult was learning to trust my instincts. Pulling up to the entry of UMASS, I knew instantly that's where I was meant to go. The campus was pretty ugly, half New England colonial, half seventies contemporary. But when I saw a girl sitting on a curb lighting a cigarette, I thought, "That will be me." I had grandiose plans of taking up smoking and dyeing my hair black, neither of which I did. My personality followed me two hundred miles to UMASS, where it turned out I was still me. So why did I feel oceans apart from myself at that Williamsburg party in my very own borough?

"There you are." I was greeted with icy eyes as a woman who was apparently the guy's girlfriend put her arm in his and pulled him away toward their circle of friends. *Um, okay. Was he flirting after all?* This happened several other times throughout the night. A guy would attempt dull conversation, and a girl would come over and claim him. *Look, I'm not trying to steal your George Michael look-alike, okay!* It was new for me, being seen as a threat to other women. We're not supposed to be enemies.

I was moping in the corner, fed up with the whole scene, when I spotted a fresh face. He stood out from the other guys in the crowd because there was nothing ironic about his outfit. He was wearing boot-legged jeans with none other than . . . boots. The rest of his ensemble suggested that he had gotten up that morning, thrown on his plaid button-down shirt, and grabbed his patterned Nordic wool sweater because that's what happened to be hanging over his chair. It all clashed in just the right way. As I'd discovered, if I wanted to talk to a guy, it was pretty simple. I just had to stand near him. This used to bother me when I went out with my girlfriends. Guys seemed to assume since we were two women together, we were two women alone, and they would often approach one of us to talk. Under the new circumstances, I used this to my advantage.

My newest target didn't seem to be meeting any girlfriend at the party, so I made my way over to where he was standing. My friend Ben, the birthday boy, approached him. Bingo. I slithered over to where they were chatting and made up an excuse to join in. Ben, not privy to my recent antics, would never suspect my motives.

"Hey Ben," I said, smiling at him and making the "I'm sorry to interrupt" expression at his friend. "Do you have any Advil or anything? I have a really bad headache."

"Yeah, I'm sure my roommate has some. Let me go check." Ben walked off toward the bathroom.

"I've got some," the handsome Nordic sweater man said. "I'm in real estate, and I've been preparing for a closing," he said, sounding important and proud. "I've been working late all week, trying to finish up by Friday so I can get out of town. Advil is a night owl's best friend."

"Where are you headed?" I asked, preemptively ordering myself to turn down any offer to join him.

"I have a house in the Hamptons, and I need to complete a project before it gets too cold to work outside," he boasted. In the past, I would have rolled my eyes at his attempt to impress me, but this time I smiled and nodded. Why was it that rich people always referred to "projects" when they talked about working on their homes? Why can't they just say, "I have to fix the toilet?"

Over the course of the night, I learned he owned the house in the Hamptons, three buildings in the city, and not one but two Land Rovers. I was a green girl at heart, but mine couldn't help but flutter a little. I would have loved a ride to the Hamptons in a big SUV. It would be so Samantha from

*Sex and the City.* "Elena, no," I reprimanded myself. I had to stay on task, and the task at hand was a one-night stand.

"How's your head?" he asked. I stepped back. Could he see me thinking too hard? "Your headache? The Advil worked?"

"Oh, yes, magically! Let's go up to the roof. I hear the view is amazing," I said, pumping myself a beer from the tap and then one for my suitor. We climbed the ladder to the roof, handing our beers back and forth to get them up there without spilling. Once on the roof, we interrupted a few other couples with the same idea and then found a corner all to ourselves. The view was indeed amazing. We could even see some stars.

"How sad it is in the city," I reflected, "that I'm excited when I can see two stars." The handsome real estate guy pulled me close to him.

"That just makes you appreciate them that much more," he whispered. And then he kissed me. Sheesh, he sure didn't wait very long. We couldn't have named a few constellations first? After a while, we ignored the drinks we had worked so hard to get up there and decided to abandon the party altogether, dashing down the ladder to leave. On the way out we ran into Ben. He looked puzzled to see me leaving with one of his friends.

"Happy Birthday!" I yelled, leaving him speechless and stunned.

In the cab, he saddled up next to me in the middle seat,

buckling his seat belt after I'd fastened my own. Did he really wear a center seat belt in the back or was he trying to impress me? I like it when people wear their seat belts. It implies they are responsible. But it doesn't matter, I reminded myself. *One-night stand, one-night stand.* I felt a wave of apprehension as we made our way to his house, far north on Riverside Drive. In the past, I'd always been cautious to the point of uptight. I never did the foolish things you were supposed to get out of your system in your twenties, like going home with a stranger.

When we arrived at his two-bedroom co-op (with a view of the Hudson), we made out as he opened the door. We made out in his impeccable kitchen, equipped with sexy German-made stainless-steel Miele-brand appliances. His house was pristine. Not a single object was out of place, which struck me as a little odd. No sweater strung over a chair?

"Wait here for a minute. I'm just going to pick up a little," he said in between kisses. Apparently his room was where he contained his mess, and apparently we were headed to his room. I took the opportunity to check out the rest of his place. There were four pairs of shoes on a rack by the door. I'd seen those shoe racks at Bed Bath & Beyond when stopping in for my replacement Brita filters. That's a good idea, I'd thought to myself. But I'm not the person who buys good ideas. I'm the person who shoves all her shoes at the bottom of her closet and can never find a matching set in a hurry. There was a framed picture of him with his family, which I took as a good sign. Add that to the list, I thought: a man who gets along with his mother. And then I shook my head, jolting my brain back into submission. It was hard to stay in the one-night-stand frame of mind. I found it did not come naturally to me, as I fought off images of us hiking and camping, he in the Timberland boots I saw parked by the door.

He returned from his bedroom just in time to rescue me from my stray daydream. Continuing where we'd left off, we kissed a bit in the living room and then along the hallway. In his room, our clothes came off quickly. He seemed to be quite comfortable with the whole one-night-stand thing, and for the most part I was too. My only hesitation stemmed from the voices in my head: *"Elena, you shouldn't be doing this."* But my actions spoke louder than my inner voice, and I reached for my stash of condoms.

"It's okay, I've got some," he said, reaching toward his nightstand. By the soft light of the moon, I was able to make out the word *Magnum* on the box he got out of the drawer. I'd been around enough to know what that meant.

He put the condom on with impressive finesse and maneuvered his way around me, lifting and twisting me this way and that. And then we were having sex. And it was good. I got really into it, feeling free like my favorite French couple. I was on top, on the bottom, on my side, leg braced against the wall, à la "the Mariola." Then, just as I was really getting into the groove, he stopped, got up, and left the room.

"I'll be right back," he yelled on his way out. I sat up, bewildered. Now what? A moment later he returned with a plastic bottle.

"What's that? Does it start with the letter *L*?" I asked, too embarrassed to say the word *lube*. I was clearly comfortable enough with him to be in his bed, so I probably should have been comfortable talking about it. But I'd always been a prude in the verbal department. Even with women, I preferred *boobs* to *tits* and *bum* to *ass*.

"Yes," he said, pumping some of the liquid into his palm. Wow! I was impressed that he was thoughtful enough to have some lube on hand. Finally, a feminist man!

And then he put it on my bum.

"That's the wrong hole!" I warned, bolting upright.

"I know," he said playfully, attempting to glide right in with his Magnum. I jumped off the bed. I wasn't necessarily opposed to the idea in general, but I was opposed to it with the real estate guy with the Nordic sweater whose last name I didn't yet know.

"I have to go," I said, and I got up to gather my clothes.

"We can just sleep," he said, turning on the light. That's actually pretty sweet, I thought, as I was pulling on my socks. Then I glanced at the night table. The bottle he'd brought in from the bathroom indeed started with the letter *L*—for Lubriderm. Hand. Lotion. I glowered at him, astonished.

"Can you please call me a cab?" I asked. He dialed a car service and accompanied me to the lobby of his building.

We sat down on the curb outside.

"This isn't how I'd imagined this turning out," he said, wrapping his arms around his knees. "I was hoping to be eating breakfast together in the morning."

"I'm sorry," I said. "This just isn't really who I am. I don't usually go home with someone I just met. I don't even know you. God, I don't even know myself these days."

"Yeah," he replied. "To think of my younger sister going home with some guy she just met makes me shudder. You really shouldn't do that, you know. It's not safe." As my cab pulled up to the curb, he mumbled the sweet send off, "Good luck with that guy!" I got in, rolled down the window, and rode home with the wind in my face.

"I THINK HE might be gay," I told Megan the following day over brunch. "His house was spotless, and he had really nice kitchen appliances," I said, feeling convincing. I leaned in closer to her. "And he wanted to have anal sex," I whispered. "On the first date, if you can even call it that."

"Or he's just a dumb rich guy with a maid," Megan replied. "How nice was his appliance?" she asked, eyebrows raised.

"He used Magnum condoms, so I guess it was big."

"You guess it was big, Elena?"

"Listen, when you've been with women for years, using any size your little heart desires, you get a bit spoiled, if you know what I mean."

"Wow, that's right. Maybe I should try women," Megan said.

"Want another reason to reconsider? Right in the middle of having sex, he got up, left the room, and returned with a bottle of *Lub-ri-derm*. Which he then tried to use as lube."

"Elena, he is definitely not gay!" Megan laughed so hard that she nearly choked on her crepe. "Gay men know to use lube. You go, Miss Lez! You went and found yourself a frat boy."

I walked home from the café feeling defeated. I was more confused than ever, yet everything was starting to make sense. My limited yet highly bizarre experiences with men helped explain why so many great women were still single in the city, and why so many others ended up with dimwits. Take Megan, for example. There you had a gorgeous, smart, successful woman who seemed to know everything there was to know about men, yet she wasted her time pining over a guy who didn't deserve her.

Their story was so cliché it was painful. I'd been Megan's ear for over two years and the scenario had barely changed. She and Jared were both successful employees in their respective positions at work, each highly sought after, in both the professional and personal sense. Megan was gorgeous inside and out, and I didn't just notice as Miss Lez. Funny and kind, at five eight (six feet in heels), her hair slicked back in a ponytail, and a mock turtleneck dress accentuating her curves, she turned everyone's eye when she walked by. She had her pick of the office staff of 150. And she picked Jared. Or rather, she was his "staff pick" during a business trip to Chicago. And though he'd since moved on, her four-inch heels were planted firmly in place.

It was the typical case of wanting what you can't have. But it was more than just that. I had witnessed too many women pining after guys who treated them like crap while there were seventeen other "nice guys" making unreturned calls. I'd done it myself, and I still couldn't solve the mystery. The last boyfriend I'd had before I met Amy was a complete mess of a man. Our courtship lasted five months, which sounds like an acceptably short amount of time to spend in a bad relationship. But it's really not, especially when it's so bad that rather than tend to you when you've just had all four wisdom teeth removed, he steals your Percocet, downs them with vodka, and then crashes and breaks your beloved vintage Schwinn (also stolen while you were sprawled out on your bed in a fog).

There was a sea of men out there, but finding a keeper, for even a one-night stand, was going to pose a challenge. Perhaps I was spoiled, having been surrounded by great men growing up. My expectations were, as Megan was constantly reminding me, too high. My dad and brother had been nothing less than a rock-solid foundation. I'd always been able to look to them for an ear, and a warm bowl of risotto, in the midst of heartache. But I seemed to be a rare breed—one of the few to have been blessed with such present, supportive male figures. I didn't have an answer for my sudden interest in men, but one thing I knew for sure was that I wasn't fishing to fill a void. I'd been fishing my entire life.

I'd protest every time, but my dad still woke me at the crack of dawn, for there were lessons to be learned, above and beyond how to tie a fly.

"Elena, I will be downstairs." His voice always grew a little stern on the third attempt to wake me. I'd drag myself out of bed, pull on some pants over my pajamas, throw on a couple more shirts, and head down to the too-bright kitchen in a sleepy stupor. My dad would be pouring hot tea into a thermos. Red Rose tea with honey and milk—a hug in a mug. The car would be packed with the fishing rod I got for Christmas and my tackle box, a birthday gift. The tackle box had failed to compete with the Barbie Dreamtime set I'd asked for (complete with matching pajamas for Barbie and me). But when it came to fishing with my dad, I'd come to forget about Barbie Dreamtime, and time altogether for that matter.

Upon devouring our breakfast of homemade oatmeal with bananas, raisins, and sunflower seeds all cooked in, we'd hop into the burgundy station wagon that somehow survived the towing of many a boat too big. As we'd pull out of the gravel driveway in the quiet of dawn, the only sounds would be the pebbles popping under the tires and our dogs barking in protest. By the time we'd reached the lake, only twenty minutes away, it would be day. Birds from every angle would be welcoming the sun, each other, and us. My dad would reverse the car onto the boat ramp. That was always my least favorite part of the excursion, second only to unpacking the car. I'd get out of the car and into the boat and hold it close to the dock as he backed the trailer into the oily water. It always looked like he'd go too far and back the burgundy wagon right into the water. Then, at what always seemed like the last possible moment, the boat would let loose and my dad would punch the gas, skidding up the ramp and off to park the car. I'd wrap the rope around the pole of the dock, just as I'd been taught, and await his return. At age eight, it was a hefty responsibility, and I felt proud. But inevitably, as I waited, I'd start to imagine the boat coming loose from the dock and drifting into the middle of the lake with me in it. It was a scary yet enthralling image. I was familiar with my dad's favorite Italian swears by then, and I would almost hear them from across the lake, as if I had indeed lost my grip on the rope and floated away.

"*Porca puttana schifa eva!*" I never did drift away.

My dad would return from parking the car with our poles in one hand and the cooler in the other, the rest of the stuff already in the boat with me. As he'd step into the boat, it would tilt precariously to one side, but I'd know how to shift my weight to help balance it out. It was an army green rowboat with a little motor and two oars (just in case). And yes, we'd had to use them.

"Porca puttana!" My dad would try starting the motor, tugging violently on the pull cord. It would always start up eventually, and he would always act as if it wouldn't. On particularly unlucky days, we'd end up using the oars, but not because the motor had died. No. Rather, it was because somehow, even from the boat, I'd manage to get my fishing line caught on a tree branch on the nearby shore.

"Porca puttana schifa!"

I never understood why, with all that open water, my dad insisted on fishing right along the shore. Apparently, that's where the fish like to hide out. Over the years, the fish certainly hid out, and I certainly learned my Italian. It was never the actual fly my dad was after, as he leaned over the edge of the boat, swatting at trees with the oar. He could have just cut the line. But my dad never cut the line. He'd stretch, sweat, and curse rather than cut the line. It was obvious, even to an eight-year-old, that he enjoyed the challenge—proving to me that you can do anything you put your mind to. Ultimately, it wasn't about catching fish anyway. I'm well aware those excursions would have been a lot easier without me in tow. But he'd invite me every time.

AFTER THE L word incident, I was ready to give up on men altogether. But being a determined Italian woman, I said, "Porca puttana" and set out on fresh water.

CHAPTER SIX

# Just-in Town for the Night

**S**tartled to find a stranger sitting in my chair at work, I walked right past my cubicle and made a beeline for Megan's desk.

"Um, Meg, there's someone in my seat. Were we bought overnight? Have I been downsized?"

"I have no idea. Ooh, let's go ask Jared. That new bimbo from HR was in his office when I got here. I need to show her who's boss."

Megan bounced out of her seat and whisked past me on her way to his office. I knew that "Let's go ask Jared" meant let Megan go ask Jared alone in hopes of an on-the-clock kiss. I sat down at her desk.

"Promoted, I see?" Noah asked, strolling by while sipping his coffee, looking rather boyish from behind his giant vente Starbucks cup.

"Promoted? I thought I was already at the top of your list." I shifted around in Megan's chair to face him. For the first time, I noticed the mole right under his left eye. It was kind of cute.

"Always. So when you want to change departments, let me know," Noah said, winking and walking away.

*Bimbo.* I hadn't heard a friend use that word in a very long time, and hearing it come out of Megan's mouth was jarring. I'd been living in a feminist lesbian bubble. My friends and I respected other women, celebrated them even. We did not see other women as rivals by default. Of course, there were bouts of jealousy here and there, friends dumped for other friends, but there lacked the general air of contempt for other women that I was witnessing in the straight world. It was not an unfamiliar concept to me, it had just been a while. There was a turning point in my teens when I realized I wasn't cut out for the divisive game of girl versus girl.

During my junior year of high school, this cute new girl, Jenny, arrived on the scene. I was threatened by her, showing up out of nowhere with her long curly auburn hair, sweet soft voice, and Kermit the Frog frame—at least that's how we referred to her, my friends and I, convinced we were fat at 120 pounds. She was one of those naturally thin girls, the ones who couldn't gain weight if they tried, as in retrospect I'm sure she'd attempted to. It was the era of fat-free foods— fat-free crackers, fat-free cookies, fat-free soups, fat-free ice cream, fat-free cheese to put on the fat-free crackers, and fat-free breakfast bars that sat in your stomach like a brick. After school I'd splurge on my low-fat "healthy" cereal of choice, Honey Bunches of Oats. I'd stuff my face, but I was always hungry. The new girl, Jenny, looked so darn good in the baggy jeans and oversize hoodies we all sported. She attracted all the guys we liked, so obviously we didn't like her.

On one particular night, she had gotten especially drunk and was writhing around on the sticky floor of the eighteen-and-over club, giggling, inviting vomit with every sudden twist of her fragile body. The industrial beats of KMFDM clashed with the faint keyboards of The Cure leaking down from the second-story dance floor. The vodka and orange juice we'd gulped down in the cleaning supply closet had gotten the best of our red-headed friend. Tonight was her night. We'd all had ours. Humiliation was our hazing into the land of Doc Martens and hair dye, where all the boys were straight edge and we girls drank ourselves into comas.

Jenny lay squirming and flirting with her unfocused eyes from her compromising position on the floor. I laughed maniacally with the cooler girls surrounding me as we summoned the guys to come and see. I was trying on "mean girl" for a change, and, not unlike my outfit, it fit several sizes too big. I couldn't help but feel guilty.

A little later in the night, I caught a glimpse of myself under the interrogating light of the girls' bathroom. I tried to block out the mirror, as well as the sound of Jenny puking in the stall behind me. Two other girls assisted her, one blocking the stall, the other holding her hair back. That's who I really am, I thought, as I faced myself in the mirror. I should be helping her. She blacked out that night. And I woke up. I would aim to be truer to myself.

Having tired of the feuds among girls, I spent most of my time with my best friend, Chuck. With a straight guy for a best friend, I didn't need to worry that we'd end up fighting over a mutual crush. (That was before I realized I liked girls, too; otherwise he would have had a run for his money.) We passed our summer days playing video games at the food court and exploring our town for new swimming holes, Naughty by Nature booming from the subwoofer of his red Honda CRX. On winter weekends we could be found hurtling down the nearby mountains on our snowboards, me racing to keep up with Chuck and his friends. The boys were competitive when it came to sports, and I preferred to let my combative nature loose on the slopes rather than the dance floor.

MEGAN RETURNED FROM her visit to Jared's office aglow.

"Jared is taking me to dinner at Pastis tonight. He had some client meeting that fell through, but he's keeping the reservation."

"That's nice dear, but what about the guy sitting at my desk?"

"Oh, I forgot to ask."

"Are you serious?" I got up and stormed away. Did it really take a mere plate of *moules frites* and a bottle of riesling to forgive two years' worth of heartache? Jared was always hot and cold, but the cold seemed so easily forgotten once the heat came back on. I understood that concept. That was how I survived New York winters. Every March I'd wonder how I could possibly live there for yet another year, and every April spring would arrive. But I didn't want to live through cold winters of the heart, even if it was "to be expected" with men.

"I guess I'm not irreplaceable after all," I joked to the stranger tapping away at my keyboard.

"Oh, hi there. Sorry, I'm just uploading some new billing software."

"That's okay, take your time. I'm not overly eager to get to my in-box."

"I'm Justin," he said, holding out his hand. "Don't worry, I won't be in your seat for long. I'm only in town for the night, to help get you guys up to speed on the new system." *Just-in town for the night. Perfetto.*

"Thank God," I said, "because I've got about a hundred client questions and not the slightest clue how to answer them."

"You and me both," he said, rolling his eyes. "I'm totally lost."

"You're telling me."

"Here, you can have your chair back. I am waiting for

this to upload anyway." He was cute—a little bit Jason Bate-man in *Arrested Development*—wearing a suit and tie, though it was hardly necessary. He looked a bit like him, too. I assumed Justin didn't don one at the corporate headquarters in Silicon Valley, where the staff was rumored to glide around "campus" on longboards in T-shirts and shorts. Even seated, I could tell he was tall. He'd had to adjust the angle of my monitor and lower my chair.

"No, no," I said. "You stay put." I pulled up a chair from the empty cubicle next door. As Justin and I were switching seats, maneuvering around in the small space, Megan walked by. She stopped and backed up to where only I could see her and started mouthing something to me. She stopped abruptly when Noah, who was one step behind her, peeked his head into my cubicle.

"Hey, where's my invite to the party?" Noah asked, clearly curious about the stranger in there with me. Just then, Jared walked in to make an announcement.

"Alright everyone, we have Gaia Media staff in town for the night, so if you don't have plans after work, I'd like you to join us at Old Town at six."

"There's your invitation right there," I said to Noah, and turned back to my training. I shooed Megan away.

Justin spent another hour at my desk, during which we exchanged horror stories of disgruntled customers: the one who left me nine voice mail messages while I was out on vacation (which my outgoing message explained), and the one who showed up at Justin's desk one day demanding a check for ad commissions.

"I don't even have the authority to write a check from the company," Justin explained to me while I laughed harder than I meant to. He grew cuter as the story progressed. My nerves were short-circuiting. When he told me the guy was escorted off campus by two security guards on Segways, I had to run to the bathroom to gather myself. There is nothing sexier to me than someone who can tell really funny stories really well. Justin was one of those people. And he was sitting in my chair at work.

The end of the day took forever to arrive. It was Thirsty Thursday, and we were all antsy to get to Old Town to take advantage of the free food and drinks. I was eager for secret reasons of my own. Noah stopped by my desk on his way to the door.

"Walk you out?"

"Oh, why not?" I was feeling unfettered.

"Ah, a step in the right direction!"

"Don't get your hopes up. I'm just trying to beat the rest of these peeps to the elevator. I'm hungry," I said.

My phone rang. It was TJ. I debated whether or not to answer. I hadn't spoken to her in several days. It rang twice more. And then I pressed "reject."

Twelve of us crammed into the elevator. I was nervous to

see Justin at the bar, so I distracted myself by estimating the combined weight of my coworkers and comparing it to the elevator limit. I bet that was the last thing on anyone else's mind, but I had always worried too much, and with my new double life underway, I was even more anxious than usual. On the nights that I actually slept soundly enough to dream, I'd been having a recurring nightmare:

"Traitor!" yells a voice from the audience. Ashton Kutcher pulls me into a passionate kiss, sending my Miss Lez crown sailing across the stage. People are pointing at me. The crowd awaits my response, but my lips won't move and I wonder what I would say if they did. Behind Ashton's head, I see TJ in the audience. I wave to her. She turns her back. I awake in a pool of sweat.

Justin was nowhere to be found at the bar, so I poured a beer from the communal pitcher and sequestered myself in a dark booth. Noah showed up a moment later, as predicted, and not halfway through my third sip, Justin joined us with a platter of pigs in a blanket. Good dog. Men are so simple. In my experience, a woman might have taken much longer to walk over, first having some fun with a few subtle signals. Although we typically refer to men as the players, I think women are more adept at the game. We are sneaky and stealthy and wise. Men just stumble right up to bat. I was going to have to employ my own wily ways if I was to flirt with Justin without Noah noticing. I reached over Justin and popped a mini-dog into my mouth. Taking someone's food without asking is a sure sign of flirtation.

"I thought you didn't eat meat," Noah joked.

I smirked at him and stole another one. Noah had to keep quiet or he'd ruin everything. Thankfully, Megan and Jared sat down at our table to add a distraction.

An hour into the evening, everyone was a bit buzzed and the bartender had turned up the music. Megan was at the bar, trying to hold Jared's attention while another woman ordered a drink and smiled at him. Noah got up to go to the restroom. Now's my chance, I thought.

"I'm still hungry. That was just an appetizer. Have you ever had a New York burger? My favorite place is a few blocks away."

"I'm not sure how a New York burger differs from burgers in L.A., but you have me intrigued," Justin said.

"What I mean is, it's not going to be a tuna burger with avocado and wasabi aioli like you Californian lightweights are accustomed to. I doubt you can even finish a whole one."

"Can you?"

"Never failed to."

I didn't bother to say goodbye to Megan and Jared, who were flirting at the bar, their faces almost touching. I was nearly running down the street toward the burger place, afraid Noah might look outside for me. Justin grabbed my arm and stopped abruptly on the sidewalk.

"Do you have any idea how gorgeous you look right now?" *Uh oh.* The flirting had worked. His boldness took me by surprise. I smiled. It was so cold that I could see our breath in the small space between us. Justin shivered a little bit.

"Come on, L.A." I pulled him toward the restaurant.

Justin impressed me by finishing his burger first. Then he got up and walked around the table to occupy the empty seat next to me. He put his arm around me and kissed my neck as I stuffed down the last few bites of mine. I wriggled in my seat, uncomfortable with our public display of affection. What if someone I knew walked into the restaurant? McHale's was rumored to be closing for good, so everyone was making what might be their last visit. I struggled to swallow the last bite, already full from the bar food. Justin excused himself to the men's room and paid for our dinner on the way past the host station. I slunk into my seat and unfastened the top button of my pants. I was pretty sure that was a no-no on a first date, but I wasn't exactly a traditional girl to begin with.

"Oh my God, I'm so full," I said when Justin returned from the bathroom.

"I'm actually shocked that fit inside you." I had a flashback of the Magnum man. I needed some air. "My hotel is around the corner. You can crash there till the fries wear off."

"Did they include Tums among your complimentary toiletries?"

We arrived at his hotel, where he went to search for the

antacids. I promptly passed out on his bed, facedown, fully clothed down to my shoes.

When I awoke the next morning, I was discombobulated. The curtains were not my own. Then I realized that I had fallen asleep in Justin's hotel room. There was a blanket and pillow on the armchair next to the bed, implying that he had slept there. He was just stepping out of the shower.

"Hey!" I yelled over the exhaust fan in the bathroom. "Get in your bed so you can at least enjoy an hour or two of real sleep."

Justin crawled into the bed next to me. We lay together, pretending to sleep. I opened one of my eyes to peek at him and he was looking right at me. I leaped on him and we started to kiss. He unraveled my scarf as I wriggled out of my five layers and foraged in my bag for a condom. I put it on him like a pro, and then we were having sex. Yes! I let out a moan of pleasure and began to gyrate along with him, high on the thrill of it. *Sex in the morning! It's my favorite! This is fun! I rock the casbah! I am unstoppable!* I sang the chorus to Nelly Furtado's new hit in my head, though I barely knew the lyrics.

*"She's a man-eater make you da da, make you da da, make you want all, all of her love."*

"Don't move!" Justin yelled, his tone frantic. I froze in place (on top of him). In broad daylight, questions flooded in along with the blinding rays of the morning sun. What just happened? Do I just stay here? Do I get off? (Apparently not.) Did I do something wrong? I assumed something had gone terribly awry, but I didn't know what, and I wasn't about to ask. Justin didn't offer any hints. He rolled out from under me, got up, and went to the bathroom without saying a word. When he did finally speak, it was only to cheerfully change the subject, if there had been one to begin with.

"Hey that Jared's a pretty cool guy, huh?" Justin asked from the bathroom.

"He's alright. He's, you know, a boss," I said, looking around the room for answers. Did that really just happen? And were we really not talking about it? All sorts of strange things happened during sex all the time, from noisy air pockets to mortifying malfunctions of varying kinds. I was accustomed to sharing a laugh with women, as we could usually relate to each other's mishaps. I was ready to address the situation with empathy and a little lighthearted humor, but something told me to keep my mouth shut. Maybe it was the fact that I knew most men to carry around deep wells of shame built up of painful issues they don't address. Or perhaps it was that he was already enthusiastically looking up the YouTube video he'd mentioned earlier in the evening.

"This guy is for real. I did some research," he said, pulling up a clip of a man barking like a dog. I shared a few of my own favorites—funny cats, Tavi's H&M rap, and the *Sex and the City* clip where Carrie falls in Dior. We ordered room service and cracked up over eggs and toast. Sometimes laughter really is the best medicine.

"Hey, why don't we share a taxi? I'll have it swing by the office on my way to the airport," Justin suggested, packing up his suitcase.

"It's probably better if we aren't seen together," I said wearily, imagining the look on Noah's face if he were to see us pull up in a cab. "But if I don't get the boot, maybe I'll see you sometime for more training."

"Here's my number. Call me," he said, handing me his card. I got dressed, gave him a hug, and left. The hotel staff was so nice, everyone singing, "Good morning, Miss" on my way out. They were probably trained to do so, so that people having affairs feel fantastic upon leaving their establishment and thus don't associate the place with the guilt that later ensues. I felt like a scandalous movie star. As soon as my feet hit the pavement, I called Keith. I had questions. He didn't answer, and I knew he'd call back two months later. That was just his way. The next best person was TJ, not that she would do anything but make fun of me. She didn't pick up either. Megan would be at her Pilates class. I was desperate. I called the only other person who knew of my secret straight capers: my brother. Of course, I wouldn't go into detail, but at least he might offer some insight into the male psyche.

"Why on God's green earth are you calling me at 8:27

a.m.?" My brother, a DJ and known to party until dawn, was prone to sleeping past noon.

"Little brother! I can't believe you picked up. I thought for sure you'd be sleeping."

"I was."

"You love me. Listen, I need some advice."

"Yes, all guys are assholes, go back to women. Goodnight."

"No wait! I know, I know, and I don't disagree with you. But I'm stubborn. I got this from Nonna Dina. And now I've started something, and it's like a puzzle I want to solve."

"Might I suggest a game of Tetris?"

"Meet me at Souen for ramen tonight. Please?"

"I get off work at nine. See you there, Sis. You're treating."

"Of course!"

I took my time walking to work, overthinking in my undercaffeinated trance. I wasn't impressed with how my man trial was panning out. How much more was I willing to sacrifice? And what exactly was to be gained? I stopped into Starbucks for a grande Awake tea. There was a long line, which added to my frustration, for I didn't really like to frequent Starbucks, opting instead for independently owned cafés when possible. But it was all Midtown had to offer. The man in front of me whipped open his *New York Times* and folded it into four easily manipulatable parts with seamless expertise. He probably did it every morning in that very spot while waiting to order his usual, a double

Americano with room for milk. I caught myself automatically leaning over to see if he was wearing a wedding ring. Where did I learn to do that? As I was no longer seeing men as mere specks in my peripheral vision, it turned out I had very well-rounded taste. Practically any seemingly single, seemingly sane guy looked really good to me. I felt a little out of control. I nearly stepped into oncoming traffic while adjusting the string of my tea bag. A cab blared at me, jolting me back up onto the sidewalk. I made my way to The Gap, the only store open at 8:00 a.m.—a practical tidbit Megan had covered in my training.

I essentially sleep-worked through my day in my new pin-striped shirt until it was finally time to meet my brother. He was late, which was nothing new. We'd set a time to meet, I'd get there early, and he'd show up just shy of an hour late. You'd think I'd have learned to give him a fake time; seven when I really meant eight.

"Hey Al." My brother scowled at me as he took his seat in the birch-wood booth. Al was his childhood nickname, assigned by my parents and short for "always late." He hated it, so I made sure to use it often.

"I'm so sorry, Sis. This DJ came in right when we were closing up, and he wouldn't stop talking." My brother worked at a DJ equipment and record shop. A chatterbox himself, I had a hard time imagining that he played a completely passive role in the conversation. But I wasn't mad. I was used to his tardiness. One might even say it's part of his charm. But I wouldn't go so far.

"It's fine, Bro, but I ordered for you. I hope you're in the mood for veggie kombu with curry." I asked my brother to catch me up on work and his latent crush on a girl who worked at a pastry shop up the street. He'd been talking about her for weeks. Little progress had been made toward a first date, but in the meantime, he was the lucky recipient of many free treats.

"Why don't you just go in there and ask her out?" I suggested.

"No, I don't want to act just like every other guy," he said.

"What do you mean?" I slurped up my scalding noodles with chopsticks. "Of course, I have my own theories, but I want to hear it from you."

"Well, for example, I don't know if the pastry girl is feeling me or not. She might be into the flirtation but not want anything more than that. Or she might be annoyed that I haven't asked her out yet. I have no idea. But of the two options, I'd rather err on the safe side than have this nice vibe between us turn sour because I ask her out and she's like, 'Oh great, another dude who can't just come in and have a pleasant exchange with me without assuming that means I want to get with him.'"

"That's true," I said, perusing the dessert menu.

"And besides, I don't get caught up in the quick strike

approach. If something is worth waiting for, I can be patient. It's more about subtly planting seeds—not the impregnating kind, more like smiles that may lead to something more. But if they don't, smiles aren't a bad thing to be spreading around, right? Plus, you've had those éclairs. They're kind of off the chain. I don't want to burn that bridge!"

"Yeah, they are. In fact, can we go there now? None of the desserts on the menu sound appealing."

"Oh hell no. I just went in there yesterday. I never go two days in a row."

I sighed and closed my menu, as well as the topic of men. My brother wasn't going to be any help. He's more of a girl than I am.

CHAPTER SEVEN

# The German Girl

I t was perfect timing when I received an invitation to an all-girl holiday party. A friend I had met at one of my brother's many DJ gigs had rented out a section of Flute, a champagne bar in the Gramercy area of Manhattan. That neighborhood normally got on my nerves, with its beautiful gated park accessible to residents only. I'd walk around the fence now and then hoping for an open door, feeling like a teenager trying to find an adult to buy me beer. But in the case of the all-girl holiday party, going to that part of town made me feel fancy. A bunch of girls getting dressed up for some dancing and celebrating of the holiday season without the distraction of men—just what the doctor ordered following my flurry of dating fiascos. And since all the girls were straight, there would be no temptations for Miss Lez either. I was looking forward to a night of jolly frolicking, free of the stresses of sexual tension.

I bought a new dress for the occasion—a layered black mesh fabric cut just above the knee, with lace trim running along the low neckline. I paired it with my favorite vintage leather boots, relieved to assemble the quirky combination without wondering if it was the "right" thing to wear. I'd become overly conscious of my ensembles, thinking way too much about what guys might or might not find attractive. I'd been doing some undercover research, asking the opinions of my male coworkers under the guise of proving men's inferiority to women. They were used to it.

"Noah, do men have a preference for long or medium-length hair on women?"

"Ah! I knew you'd come around."

"You wish. I'm just curious. I may be batting for the other team, but we play the same game." Noah leaned on the edge of my desk.

"Well, we probably notice three lengths: There is hair so short you look like a boy. Shoulder-length hair is good for pulling a bit. Then there is hair down to your ass, which will take too long to get ready and will undoubtedly get in the way. Everything in between is the same haircut just grown out." It couldn't be possible that guys didn't notice the difference after a $200 trip to the hair salon. Over lunch one day, I decided to dig deeper. What other wisdom might Noah impart to me as he attacked his Chipotle burrito?

"Noah, today's topic: shoes. What do men really like?"

I was curious, because I mistrusted Megan's claim that men preferred heels. Instead I leaned toward the theory that the confidence I gained by being able to walk outweighed the sex appeal of an extra few inches.

"Shoes?" Noah took a chug of his Coke. "They cover your feet. Like hair, they come in three types. There are flat shoes you can run in, heels that make your legs look hot, and boots for rain and snow. We may notice the difference between red, black, and white shoes, but there are no middle shades. Baubles, bells, and decorations, you can be certain we don't see."

I took notes on my napkin. *Shoes: boots fine, colorblind*

"Okay then, what about lingerie?" I asked, boldly crossing into suggestive territory.

"What, like what color should it be?"

"Yeah, I guess. And does it make a difference whether it's expensive or not?" I'd seen some decent-looking lingerie in the window of Joyce Leslie for only $14.99.

"Honestly, I think we couldn't care less what it looks like. I've had many women ask me what kind of lingerie I like most. It's like wrapping paper on a Christmas present, and men are like kids. We can't wait to rip it off and get to the fun part. So yeah, you look hot in it. Amazing in fact. But we notice that the package is wrapped, not the pattern on the paper."

*Lingerie: cheap*

"And while we're on the topic," Noah outlined my outfit with his finger in the air. "I can't stand the latest dress-over-jeans fad. Don't put on jeans that flaunt your ass and make it look great and then cover it up with a tent. I mean, it's different for you because you're not trying to attract dudes, but this mix-and-match style drives men crazy. And another thing," Noah continued (clearly I'd unleashed the dragon). "Don't yell at us for checking you out in spandex and running gear. You are actually naked save for a two-millimeter layer of clothing. What do you expect us to do? Men check out women as more of a pastime, perhaps the way women window-shop for shoes. We're thinking, *Oh, that looks nice,* and then it's out of our mind as we move on to the next person walking down the street. In no way does it mean we're not satisfied in our relationship. I look at women and cars the same way."

"Alright then, what exactly are you guys looking for then? In a relationship?" I asked, perched on the edge of my seat.

"What dudes are really looking for is a girl that looks hot on Sunday morning in sweatpants and a hoodie. Anyone can put on makeup and nice clothes and look great. We want a girl who looks sexy while she is helping us paint the house. All we really want to do is eat, sleep, do a little work that makes us feel manly, have fun, and do it all over again. And we sure as hell don't need to fill silence with words. A ride with my guy friends to the beach equals loud music, an occasional funny story, and a grunt here and there. We give one-word answers, pound fast food, slurp down sodas, and arrive. A ride with my girlfriend is exhausting. I feel like we have to throw the conversation ball back and forth from the time I start the car until I put it in park. You females are always criticizing men for being simple. The thing is, we never argued with you!"

"Noah?" I asked, leaning back, smiling and twirling my pen in my hand.

"Yeah?"

"Don't use the word *female* as a noun."

SINCE I'D RECENTLY learned that women appreciate each other's outfits more than men do, I was excited to once again get decked out for the girls.

By the time I arrived at the party, the other women were already tipsy, refilling each other's flutes with Veuve before their glasses were even empty. Apparently, we were all overdue for a break from men. The gracious host walked around offering hush puppies to her guests, playfully serving them off the mound of cleavage pouring out of her dress. Our private party area was sectioned off from the rest of the bar by thick red velvet curtains. Since there were no men at the party, there was a relaxed, playful feeling in the room. It felt like I was in the dressing room at the strip club where my friend used to work. Hidden from the male gaze, the girls would compliment each other's outfits and fluff each other's hair in an air of camaraderie.

"Who makes your dress?" asked a voice with a thick accent, German I suspected. I turned to face a gorgeous girl in a beautiful dress. She had a cast on her hand, which she'd attempted to cover with a matching silk wrap.

"Oh, it's Weston Wear," I said, "my favorite designer from San Francisco. She was a dancer and therefore makes clothes you can actually move in." I did a little wiggle to demonstrate.

"I like it," she said, running her fingers through the fabric. "But this type of clinging fabric does not work so well on me."

"I see you two have met," the hostess said, bounding over with a bottle of bubbly. "Annika and Karoline are designers, and I think you'd really like their stuff. This is one of theirs," she said, spinning around and bending over to showcase the open back of her dress.

"It's beautiful," I said. Annika grabbed the bottle and filled my glass to the brim.

"I need someone to keep up with me," she said. "I am trying to numb the pain." She held up her arm with the cast and frowned.

"Yeah, what happened there?" I asked.

"Pole dancing incident."

"Oh." I drank a generous gulp from my glass.

"Karoline and I are taking classes, and I attempted some little stunts I should not have. I was trying to gracefully slide down the pole upside down and then lusciously drip myself into a chair. Let's just say I received many black and blues, and Karoline almost had a heart attack."

Just then her friend walked up and joined the conversation.

"This is Karoline," Annika said. Karoline reached out her hand to shake mine.

The three of us chatted about clothes, a topic I never grow tired of. I could add designer to the list of things I've wanted to be. Their inspiration: sixties hippie meets layperson pole dancer. The result: long, bodice-hugging blouses (or short dresses if you dared, which apparently Paris Hilton did) thrown over jeans and topped off with, you guessed it, tall vintage boots. We made a natural trio and posed as Charlie's Angels for the host's flashing camera.

As the night wore on, women started to forgo glasses altogether and instead drink champagne straight from the bottle. There was a charge of sexual energy in the room; the vortex the host, who pranced around snapping sexy photos. Women grabbed each other's waists and pressed their chests together, puckering up to make kissy faces for the camera. Annika and I talked and laughed at the perimeter of the party, taking turns to stock up on double helpings of hors d'oeuvres.

Suddenly there was a roar of cheering. I looked up to see two straight girls lip-locked under a piece of mistletoe someone was dangling above their heads. They were full on making out, French style (and not the bonjour kiss on each cheek). A circle formed around them, and the host's camera flashed continuously, creating a strobe light effect. Two other women replaced the first ones and after that two more. It was a game of spin the bottle without the bother of the bottle (though there would have been plenty to choose from, based on the amount of champagne that had clearly been consumed).

"Kiss her, she's Miss Lez!" the host yelled, pointing at me and shoving a woman in my direction. I nearly spit my drink onto the floor. I laughed nervously and refused the tempting offer, holding my hand up and shaking my head. But I had little choice, as I was outnumbered. I was pulled into the circle with force. The next thing I knew I was kissing somebody. I couldn't see who it was in the craze of the worked-up crowd, but I knew it was a woman because her face was lusciously soft. After a few seconds, I tore myself away, giggling along with the rest of the girls, floating on their contagious high of rebellion. *What the heck is happening?* They fought over who got to kiss me next. As Miss Lez, I was a novelty. I retreated back to my place near Annika.

"Miss Lez?" Annika said.

I described the pageant and gave Annika the lowdown on my recent antics, but she was not very interested in my stories about men.

"What is it like, being with a woman?" Annika asked, linking her arm in mine. I stood there stunned, overcome with shyness in her presence. My state of ease had gone poof with the new notion that straight girls can go gay when drunk, like gremlins when fed after midnight (only good). I had watched that terrifying movie during a slumber party with friends in fourth grade, and come to think of it, that party had unfolded quite like this one.

My friend Andie, an only child, was allowed to have eight girls over for the night. Her dad worked for a major record label and thus always had the newest in media technology, including, somehow, a copy of *Gremlins* on VHS the very year it came out. We'd all brought our coolest pajamas for the party: *Flashdance* T-shirts and flannel pants with strawberry or flower prints. We bounced around on the bed, screaming and grabbing each other during the scariest parts of the movie. As soon as the credits were rolling, Andie shut off the movie and put on Madonna's "Like a Virgin" video, of which she also magically had a copy. We started dancing around the room, imitating Madonna's dance moves, rewinding the tape at the end and replaying it repeatedly.

"Let's play married!" Andie said, grabbing another girl. They kissed with closed lips, as if in a film from the thirties. We howled and clapped. Andie's party was the best of the year, and also the last. The following week, one of the nuns (did I mention I went to a Catholic school?) made a phone call to Andie's mother. The school had received a complaint from a girl's parents. Someone at the party had told on us. I will never know whether it was the dirty dancing or the gruesome movie that was deemed the more heinous offense. In either case, there were no more parties at Andie's house.

"I KISSED MY friend in high school, but it was weird," Annika said. *Oh my God, she is flirting with me.* She touched my shoulder while asking her questions and looked me straight in the eye. *Uh oh.* She was sexy and adorable at the same time, bearing the kind of natural beauty that looks almost alien when enhanced by makeup. And she seemed to know it, her big blue eyes framed only by her platinum blond hair and the slightest hint of mascara. She didn't need lipstick. Her full lips were naturally rosy, so much so that I bet she got annoyed with how red they were all the time. I had a friend like that in college. Her nickname was Rosie because she always had pink cheeks and lips, though she never wore an ounce of makeup. It bothered her, but I'd always been envious of her supposed problem. Like my mom's, my own lips take on a slightly blue hypothermic hue when nude. Thus I inherited my mom's lipstick addiction, too.

I had to pull myself together. But Annika's questions were especially charming when asked in that accent of hers. And then she came closer to whisper in my ear.

"Ehlehnah. Everyone got to kiss but us."

"Don't worry, we will," I said with affected conviction. I was accustomed to being courted, femme on the streets and in the sheets. But as Miss Lez, I needed to take charge. Or so I thought. Annika grabbed me and ordered in her German monotone, "Come home to my house with me."

The women hooted and hollered as Annika and I

ditched the party together. Her long hair brushed my neck as she whipped herself into the cab. I ducked in and she recited her address to the driver. We were Harlem-bound. Harlem was far enough from my house in Brooklyn that I knew I wasn't going to make it home that night. And that was just fine. No part of me was hesitant, getting into the cab with Annika. I didn't have the same little knot in my gut that I'd had with the guys. If anything, in her presence I felt protected. Flying up the Palisades Parkway in our yellow chariot, the snow-covered city was a magical land, lit up by sparkly decorations and infused with holiday cheer. Or maybe it was the champagne.

And then we were kissing. In the cab! I was a little bit embarrassed because I'd never been big on public displays of affection. But I was sure the cabbie had seen it all before, and for that matter, much, much more.

We kissed outside her apartment door and then she unlocked it and pushed me inside. Clothing racks lined the hallways, jammed full of her fashions. It was an endless labyrinth of earth tones, my favorite. *I can't wait to share clothes!* Like mine, her apartment was sweltering.

"I'm sorry it is so hot in here. I have no way to control it," she said, opening the windows wider.

"Are you kidding? I love it. I'm always cold."

"Me, too!"

I went into the bathroom and washed my hands with

the same Peaceful Patchouli soap I used at my house. I felt right at home.

Just inside her bedroom door, Annika pulled me toward her bed and we fell onto a mountain of the softest sheets ever, the kind that feel like whipped cream. *Note to self: thread count counts.* And speaking of soft, her skin felt like silk compared to the men I'd been with. Typically the more passive one when in bed with someone new, I leaped out of my comfort zone and on top of her, assuming I would have to lead the way.

"I want to do you," she said in the same monotone with which she'd given her address to the cab driver. And then she flipped me around, pinning my arms to the bed.

"Are you sure you haven't done this before?" I asked.

The thing about being with women is that it doesn't really matter how much experience either one has under her belt (in Annika's case, none), because what's under her belt is the same as mine. It's much easier to steer the ship when you're familiar with the helm. Needless to say, it was awesome. And then we slept with our arms and legs intertwined.

The next morning I awoke to the sun streaming through the plants hanging in her bedroom window. *I want to wake up here every day.* There were sounds coming from the kitchen. I wrapped myself in a patchwork quilt and headed to the bathroom.

"Good morning. Would you like tea?" Annika asked through the door.

"Yes, please!"

"And use my toothbrush if you don't mind."

I smiled at myself in the mirror as I brushed my teeth with the familiar flavor of the same fennel toothpaste I used at home. I didn't mind at all sharing her toothbrush. The bristles weren't faded and frayed like the guys' toothbrushes I'd been seeing as of late. How funny, I thought. All of that silly experimentation with men and I found myself back with a girlfriend in the end. (I'd already decided that Annika was mine.)

In the kitchen, I took a chair at the table and watched as she struggled to make tea with one hand, her hand with the cast at her side, wrapped in another pretty fabric.

"Let me help you with that," I said, laughing.

"No, I've got it. Drink your juice."

The glass of organic orange juice she had placed on the table in front of me glowed in the warm December morning light. And then Annika came over, placed our mugs of tea on the table, and squatted next to me, resting her hand on my thigh.

"I had a lovely time last night," she said sweetly. I braced myself for the follow-up letdown, expecting her to say, "But I'm straight." Instead she just stayed there looking up at me, smiling. And so I smiled back.

"Me, too."

As I was applying my makeup in the bathroom, Annika came in and wrapped her arms around my waist from behind.

"I want to watch you make your eyes."

I proceeded to apply my graphite eye shadow and jet-black liner as she watched in the mirror, resting her chin on my shoulder.

"This is all you do for the smoky look?" Annika asked. "I was taught to always wear mascara with eye shadow."

"No, it's better without," I said, turning around to face her. "Close your eyes."

I put a faint layer of shadow on her lids and handed her the liner to apply herself, for fear of poking her eye out.

"Yes," she said, assessing herself in the mirror. "But I think I need mascara. I have no eyelashes."

"Oh stop," I said, grabbing her. "It looks great."

"It looks better on you." She pinched my cheek and wriggled away.

"I need to get dressed for work. Wait for me and we will take the train together." Everything Annika said sounded more like an order than a request. I loved it.

I went back into the kitchen and starting doing her dishes. There was quite a big pile. It must have taken her twice as long as usual to wash them with the cast on.

"Stop that!" she yelled from her bedroom.

"Too late!"

It felt nice to do her dishes for her. If she had been a man, washing the dishes might have taken on a whole different meaning. I know myself. I would have thought too much about it. I'm doing his dishes. Does this mean I am falling into some subordinate domestic role? But he's got a broken hand. It's a nice thing to do. But I don't want to set some sort of precedent. And so on. With Annika, I didn't think at all. I just dried each plate with her retro Niagara Falls dish towel and inspected the pictures taped to her refrigerator: friends, family, and several postcards from tropical places. A girl after my own (cold hands) warm heart.

She emerged from her room covered head to toe in hues of burgundy and brown. On the way to the front door, she slipped into her bulky UGG boots and topped off her outfit with a signature hand-knit hat from her clothing line.

"Pick one," she said, holding the basket in front of me.

"Really?"

"I think this one will look super cute on you." She handed me a beige hat with an embroidered flower.

"Wow, thank you. Are you sure?"

"You did my dishes, Elena. Yes I am sure."

I leaned in to kiss her as she was reaching for her keys. It was one of those awkward moments where you realize halfway into it that your timing is off, but it's too late to turn back. She looked up just when my lips were about to land on hers. We kissed for a brief moment, but it was weird the way daytime kisses can sometimes be, even with people you've been dating for years. One person is prepared for it, while the other is wondering where their cell phone is.

On the subway, she placed her hand on my thigh again, which I found very brave for a straight girl. *Maybe it's because she's European,* I thought as I looked around. My fear of homophobic people had become habitual over the years. I wish I could say I was one of those people who say "Fuck it" and let people stare if they want to. But I had grown very afraid of hate. I'd had enough friends beaten up, even in such progressive places as San Francisco and New York, to warrant the concern I carried everywhere like a handbag.

The woman across from us was zoning out in our direction, but otherwise the people of New York were reading their papers and fondling their phones. No one cared that two women had just woken up in the same bed, totally smitten with each other. I put my hand on Annika's.

"Here," she said, handing me a card. "This is my phone number. The next stop is mine."

I took the card and put it in my coat pocket next to the tea bag tag I'd taken from her kitchen. I wanted to buy the same cardamom Ceylon so that I could start every day just as deliciously. Then I took out a pen, wrote my number on her cast, and drew a heart around it. I am such a dork.

As the train screeched into Times Square, she leaned over and kissed me on the cheek. I squeezed her hand and held onto it as she attempted to exit.

"Ah!" she yelped, laughing and tugging away from me. She jumped out the door just as it was closing. I smiled, pulled out my cell phone, crossed my legs, and pressed "play" on the *Wheel of Fortune* game I'd downloaded earlier in the week. A message popped up:

"Attention: Your free trial will expire in 1 day(s)."

# CHAPTER EIGHT

# The Business Trip

I t was just as well that a business trip took me to L.A. to train at our West Coast office, because it stopped me from willing Annika to call. It had been three weeks since I'd left her a voice mail. When I hadn't received a call back, I'd sent an email as well. And when two more days passed with no response, I cursed myself for sending it. With not one but two methods of follow-up floating out there in limbo, there was no room for an ounce of doubt. I was being dissed.

I was really in for it. I already knew I didn't know much about men. But women? Women at least called back. I resisted the urge to contact our mutual friend, the party host. As shocked as I was not to hear back from Annika, the answer was crystal clear. I could already hear my friend's voice on the other end of the line: "Elena, what did you think would happen? Annika is straight." I should not have been so surprised, but I was. She'd been so sweet with me, and so present. There was the minor detail of her sexual orientation, but I'd seen greater obstacles overcome. My technologically inept father had learned how to use email. Why couldn't I have a straight girlfriend?

I conferred with Megan during lunch one day, guessing she'd have a more accurate perspective than Miss Lez. Jabbing at our chopped salads at a little restaurant near the office, I recounted the story of meeting Annika and going back to her house. I made sure to include all the pertinent details, like how sweet she had been the morning after and how she had left me her phone number.

"So what happened, Meg? Did she get scared?"

"Girl, there are so many possible answers. But yes, she probably freaked out."

"Tell me this then. If you suddenly found yourself interested in a woman, what would you do?" I asked.

"Well, I've had crushes here and there, like when I found myself getting way too frequent haircuts from my hot Shane look-alike hairdresser."

"Shane? Like from *The L Word* Shane?"

"Yeah."

"You watch that show?"

"Oh yeah. All my friends watch it, too, and we would all turn for Shane. Even my mom has a crush on her."

"Your mom watches it, too?"

"Anyway, yes, I can find other women attractive, and I might even do something if I were drunk enough. But a kiss at the back of a bar is a far cry from taking a woman to a wedding as my date. I don't think I'm cut out for that."

"Oh God, she's never going to call."

"Well, you said she's a designer, right? It's fashion week soon, so maybe she got really busy with work."

"Too busy to pick up the phone?"

"Elena, I'm trying to help you stay hopeful. Even I would rather see you with a woman. This whole thing was fun at first, but I think you've got even worse luck with men than I do."

Megan's comment made me anxious. I was frustrated, and determined to prove her wrong. So I did something very, very bad. After having turned him down incessantly for years, I extended an offer to Noah for an after-work drink.

"Noah, you, me, happy hour, my treat?" He didn't answer at first. "To thank you for giving me all that input on men," I said. He just stood in front of me with his mouth gaping open. "You'd better take me up on this right now, because I'm about to change my mind."

He was quiet as the two of us descended in the elevator alone.

Over two-for-one beers at a hipster dive bar near the office, we discussed work, sports, and his recent breakup. I offered the female perspective.

"Yes, she probably broke up with you because you turned down her offer to spend Christmas with her family. Yes, even though she said it was no big deal, it really was. Yes, by turning down the offer, you essentially said you are not that serious about her, and she dumped you to find someone who is."

Halfway through the third round of drinks, I returned from a visit to the ladies' room to find him reading Nietzsche at the bar. I burst out laughing. The book was huge, and he must have lugged it around with him everywhere, just waiting for opportunities to impress girls.

"Noah," I said. "Really?"

He put the book away, embarrassed. I melted at the sight of him sitting there looking so vulnerable. Without thinking, and to make up for teasing him, I leaned over and kissed him right there at the bar. He was so shocked by my seemingly spontaneous straightness that he barely kissed me back and instead nearly fell off his stool. Had he been all talk all that time? It was beginning to seem that when women take control, men don't know what to do with themselves.

"Sorry," I said, laughing. "That just happened." Noah looked like a deer in headlights. We paid our tab and walked outside, where I hailed a cab, took Noah home with me, and had my way with him. The poor guy didn't know what hit him, and before either of us could catch our breath, I was calling another cab.

"Damn," he sighed, shaking his head and laughing as he pulled on his socks.

"I'm sorry, but I'm late to see my brother deejay," I said, grabbing my coat and my keys. My Miss Lez crown was vanishing from atop my dresser like Marty McFly in *Back to the Future*. When we pulled up to the concert venue, I jumped out of the cab and blew Noah a kiss. His hair was all mussed and he looked flustered as he gave the cab driver his address and continued uptown. I was officially out of control. And I was kind of scaring myself. Noah never told a soul. I must have scared him, too. Every once in a while at work, he'd say, "Hey, let's do that again," and I would just smile and say, "Do what?"

ON THE PLANE to California for the training, I watched endless episodes of *Seinfeld* and ate the entire box of Triscuits I'd brought "to snack on." By the time we landed, I had that gross carb- and oil-infused, bloated, dehydrated feeling that I associate with flying. I couldn't wait to get to my hotel room and shower. As happened every time I traveled for work, the hotel reception desk did not have the credit card authorization my company was supposed to have sent. This meant that I had to hand over my personal credit card and would inevitably wait forever to get reimbursed.

I was trying to hide my irritation when my coworker Carlos walked in. Carlos worked with me in the finance department, and his sunny disposition remained intact even through a cross-country flight. I was cheered up by the sight of him. We'd become close over the years, though our personal paths never crossed, save for his wedding, which he'd invited me to. It was the craziest party I'd ever been to in my life, surpassing all the UMASS ragers. The dancing commenced before the cake even came out and continued well after dawn. I faked my way through the salsa and merengue with his flirtatious four-foot-four dad. When Carlos returned from his honeymoon, I was still nursing my hangover. And according to him, his was on the tamer side of Puerto Rican weddings.

"E-Money!"

"Carlos! Hey, they don't have the company card on file, so we have to use our own."

"Oh snap, I was planning on maxing mine out tonight with my boys. My cousin lives out here, and we're gonna party."

"I've got your back. I'll include your room on my card."

"For real? Aw, you're the best. And for that? Drinks on me tonight."

"Tonight? That's sweet, but it's already past my bedtime in New York."

"Go get dressed, Grandma. You haven't been your perky self lately. What you need is a night on the town. Who knows, you may even meet a lucky lady. See you down here in an hour."

Normally I would have passed up the offer, curled up under the covers, and fallen asleep halfway through a pay-per-view new release. But I was at a crossroads. If I gave in to defeat, it would only be downhill from there. It was taking extra effort to laugh at people's jokes, and the slightest thing made me cry. I had been feeling vulnerable ever since meeting the German Girl. My heart felt like the big piece of blank poster board I'd brought home to make a collage for the New Year. Each year I like to make a visual reminder of the goals I wish to accomplish, to help me stay on track. As the subway transported me back home from the art store, I was doing my best to keep my bulky poster board heart out of the way of the other passengers. Even so, the snarky teenage girl next to me shifted dramatically and snarled, "Quit poking me with your board!" I glared back at her. And then I went home and cried.

For my outing with Carlos and the boys, I threw on some jeans, a tank top, a sexy necklace, and my boots. I checked myself in the mirror. Yep, I was ready either to dance or to paint a house. Perfect. Carlos was fifteen minutes late to meet me in the lobby, but I didn't mind because the hotel flaunted a perfect view of the Burbank Airport. I watched plane after plane take off and land; planes setting out on their predetermined routes, set for predetermined destinations. I envied the pilots just then, knowing exactly where they were headed and more important, why.

We arrived at the famed jazz club The Mint just in time for the early bird entry fee. When I hear *jazz club,* I imagine a crowd around my dad's age sitting around in comfy chairs surrounded by posters for even older jazz clubs, barely visible in the dim lighting. The lighting was dim, but that's about all I was right about. The crowd was more of a twentysomething range. I really was Grandma.

"E-Money, what are you going to start with?"

I let Carlos choose my drink, since I tended toward the ones with predictable effects, old lady drinks like lager and chardonnay. If I was going to loosen up, I was going to need something stiff. I clinked my Long Island iced tea with Carlos and his friends. "Cheers!"

A little later, Carlos and his cousin were in a heated debate over something involving the Dodgers and the Mets. I wandered over to the bar to order a seltzer and noticed a guy standing alone. I asked him the time, knowing full well everyone has a cell phone and every cell phone has a clock. But since I'd discovered that all you need to do to get a guy to talk to you is utter anything at all, I then said, "Boy, it's crowded in here, huh?" In my former life, I would do anything to avoid guys at a bar. However, in the midst of my MANia, the abundance of single men was working for me. And in that new city, I was clad in a confidence not my own. I was acting, like everyone else in L.A.

I let him buy me a beer and we chatted while he waited for his friends. He was much younger than me, by ten years or so. I could tell by the way he spoke to me. He was playful and sweet, lacking the polished pickup lines that seemed to come with age. Quite a few wrinkles revealed themselves around the creases of his eyes when he smiled. He was either older than he seemed, or a big-time partier. I assumed the latter, based on his Technicolor sneakers and green Puma hoodie. When Carlos fetched me to move on to the next club, I accepted the guy's phone number, just in case.

I was whisked from bar to bar, as Carlos and his friends scoured Sunset Boulevard for the happening scene. Hours past Grandma's bedtime, we landed at a strip club, where the boys just couldn't resist treating me to a lap dance.

"To cheer you up," Carlos said, pushing me toward the girls waiting to escort me to the back of the club.

Alone in the tiny room with my private dancers, I giggled nervously as they ground against my thigh.

"We're girlfriends, you know," one of the dancers said.

"I have some friends who are strippers," I replied, trying to bond with them. That was apparently a big buzz kill, as they proceeded to sway around the room, looking bored, until a Herculean bouncer came in to tell us our time was up. Back in the main room, Carlos was slipping a bill into the garter belt of one of the dancers. I wedged myself in between them to tell him I was leaving and went outside to text my last resort from the first bar. We met up for last call at a lounge club down the street, and then I took him back to my hotel room. Something had taken over me. It was like Samantha Jones had possessed the body of Charlotte York.

*Elena, what are you doing?* I watched myself slide the hotel room key card into the slot on the door. Click.

We started to kiss, and since I was still acting, I threw him down on the bed. We followed all the same steps I'd become accustomed to. He lifted off my shirt, I lifted off his, he unbuckled his belt, I slid out of my jeans. Everything was going according to plan. But then, once he was on top of me, he began thumping around at a manic pace. I tried moving with him, but our bodies banged around out of synch. I was in bed with the Energizer Bunny on speed. *Why does he have so much stamina? Is it because he's younger,* I wondered?

"I'm sorry, but I'm tired," I said, stopping.

"No, it's me. I'm sorry," he replied, "I drank Red Bulls and vodka all night."

Nice one, Elena. Somehow, all the way in L.A., I'd ended up back in college on one of those dates I'd heard about but managed to avoid until now. I swiftly saw him to the door.

High by osmosis, I opened my computer to lull myself to sleep window-shopping for shoes (shoes that would sit in my virtual cart for days until the page eventually expired). My fake shopping was a blatant distraction from the storm brewing inside. I was growing tired of my seemingly point-less escapades and was just about ready to throw in the monogrammed towel. I "bought" pair after pair of sandals. *They're on sale!* Then I checked my email. I had to rub my eyes to make sure what I was seeing was real. An email from The Yoga Teacher! It said, "Great to see you in class today!" Was he joking with me? (Perhaps.) Did he get my email wrong and somehow switch out someone else's with my own? (Odd, but slightly possible.) Did he think he saw me, but it was someone else who looked like me and for some bizarre reason he was happy to see me? (Highly unlikely.) Clearly, I should have gone right to sleep and brainstormed potential witty responses in the morning over a big hotel buffet breakfast. At least then my brain would have been awake. But instead, I wrote back immediately.

"That was my evil twin. I hear she's into yoga." Send. Then I awaited his reply. They say a watched pot never boils. A watched email in-box is like a reverse time machine. Rather than speeding into the past, the future unfolds at a pregnant snail's pace. Never mind that it was 5:00 a.m. New York time (not that I was counting). There are some things I'm too embarrassed to admit to anyone. Like that *Jurassic Park* is my favorite movie to catch on TV. Or that I still yearned for approval from The Yoga Teacher, even after everything I'd put myself through. My yearning had moved beyond the sexual. I just wanted him to think I was sane so that I could prove to myself that I was. I refreshed my in-box. Nothing. I couldn't sleep, and I couldn't stand the waiting. I needed a solid distraction, so I did the last thing on earth I should have.

The groggy receptionist at the front desk was reluctant to lend me the scissors.

"I'll bring them back, I promise." I returned to my room, wrapped myself in a towel, set up shop in the white marble bathroom, and began to cut my hair. Snip. Snip snip. I don't know how many times it will take me to finally learn that I should never, ever pick up a pair of scissors when I'm sad. It's an express train to depression. *If I just trim my bangs a tiny bit so they're cute again, I'll feel better.* Oh sure, I always like it at first, checking out my hair in the mirror from all angles. *Wow, I did a good job this time! Maybe I should go to cosmetology school!*

And then . . .

I went out into the room, watched a rerun of *Friends,* wished I hadn't cut my bangs so I could instead grow my hair out like Phoebe's, returned to the bathroom, checked my hair in the mirror, zoomed in on one stray strand longer than the others, picked up the scissors, and embarked on The Beginning of The End. There is a huge difference between a haircut by a professional and one by a lonely, overtired woman. A professional knows how to shape from the inside out, layer by layer, building upon a solid foundation so that everything falls into place. The disheartened, PMS-ing layperson technique is more like cutting into paper in kindergarten, fingers crossed that when you unfold it, it at least somewhat resembles a snowflake.

Likewise, the darkness that ensues after a bad self-inflicted haircut is like no other. It is a feeling set aside by the universe specifically for women who are feeling bad about themselves and just can't resist feeling worse. And the fact that you did it to yourself allows for endless mental flogging. *I'm so stupid. I do this every time. This is L.A. Maybe I can get extensions.*

Sleep was my only refuge from the storm stirring inside, until I awoke the next morning and looked in the mirror. Still no reply from The Yoga Teacher. 10:00 a.m. New York time. I got dressed and took extra time with my makeup to compensate for my hair. I ran into Carlos in the lobby.

"You smell like a brewery," I said, cringing. "How are you even functioning? I feel like the worm at the bottom of the tequila bottle you guys were polishing off when I left you."

"Yes, but you have to admit you had fun last night, didn't you?"

"I did." And that was all I would admit to.

I drove us over to the Gaia Media campus in our spiffy hybrid rental car. As we pulled into the parking garage, my stomach did a somersault at the sight of Justin. I'd been so distracted, it hadn't occurred to me that I might see him there. Four security checks later, Carlos and I grabbed cups of coffee and tea and made our way to the conference room. Justin fiddled with his laptop at the podium. I went up to say hello.

"Excuse me, sir. Are you leading this training?"

"Well hello there. Yes, in fact, I am."

"Great. Is there a placement test for those of us who've already had private lessons?" Justin was testing out his laser pointer and shone it in my face like a cop wielding a flashlight.

"Hmm, why don't we discuss this over dinner tonight? There's a place I know called Magnolia, corner of Sunset and Vine. Eight o'clock?"

"See you there," I said. I returned to my seat smiling.

"Hey, isn't that the guy that was in the office a while back?" Carlos asked.

"Yeah, that's him. Hey, do you have a pen I can borrow?" I wrote "magnolia sunset/vine 8" in sloppy script on the back of my folder.

I felt a little guilty for being bored to tears throughout the training, but not even Justin could make billing interesting. The number seven kept jumping out at me from his Power-Point presentation. I'd always known the number to be auspicious. Seven. Before The Adjustment, it had been seven years since I'd even looked at a man. And before that, it had been seven years since I'd gone off to college and come out in the first place. As silly as I knew it was to try to apply a theory to something as mysterious as my sexuality, I did it anyway. I made a list on my notepad:

1. The seven-year itch
2. The seven days of creation according to Christianity
3. The seven deadly sins, all of which I remembered from Catholic school (and all of which applied to me): lust, greed, sloth, wrath, envy, pride, and gluttony
4. The number of gateways traversed by Inanna during her descent into the underworld

5. Buddha walked seven steps at his birth

6. Jewish newlyweds are fed for seven days following their wedding (I always remember this one because it involves food.)

7. Harry Potter was born in July, the seventh month of the year

THE LIST, LIKE the training, went on and on, until I was back in my hotel room and it was seven o'clock. Time to leave for my date.

TJ's new ring tone went off on my way to the restaurant. I'd assigned her a motorcycle engine sound in honor of her new girlfriend, Moto Guzzi.

"I'm on my way to a date, what's up? And are you wearing a helmet at all times like you promised?"

"Is it a date with the Don't Move Guy?" No matter how many times I'd been reminded that I shouldn't tell TJ anything she might stockpile as ammo against me, I still told her everything. And she always used it against me.

"Yes. He's nice."

"Uh huh. Call me when you're done. Which shouldn't be too—"

"Goodbye."

I was early for dinner and Justin was late. I approached the empty host station.

"I suppose you're here to eat." One of the waiters glided

over, grabbed a menu from the pocket of the podium, and gave me a big smile. He was cute in that Ben Affleck way, where he looked just like every other tall, white, brown-haired aspiring L.A. actor who could either play a hip young dad or a charming single guy on a sitcom, but with a special little twinkle in his eye.

"It's what I do best. Oh, and I'll need two menus please," I said.

"You don't even know my name and you want me to have dinner with you?"

In spite of myself, I laughed. The waiter was charming, just like that guy on that sitcom. *Uh oh.*

"I have a few more hours on my shift, but I suppose I could join you for a few." The waiter straddled the chair across from me. In New York, a waiter would be fired on the spot for sitting down on the job. But California was much more laid back. So much so that the waiter reclined, leaning on the rear legs of his chair, looking quite at home.

"Why don't you earn your tip and bring me a glass of wine? A big one," I said, trying to shoo him away before Justin arrived while still maintaining the flirtation.

"You nervous about breaking up with the guy who's meeting you here?" Again, I laughed, this time a loud and boisterous roar. "Seriously, what kind of guy makes a pretty girl like you wait?"

I waited and waited, growing hungrier and more irritated

by the minute. I was accustomed to the West Coast time difference—the difference being that in New York, people (aside from my brother) were on time, and on the West Coast they were not. But when forty minutes rolled by, I rolled up my sleeves, took a deep breath, and decided to brave dining alone. Normally opposed to ordering Italian food anywhere other than Italy, upon the waiter's recommendation I opted for the fusilli Bolognese. It was out of this world. Ten points for good taste. The waiter, whose name I learned was Paul, kept me company by popping by every few minutes to refill my already full water glass or to drop off a free treat. As I was picking out my dessert, I received a text from Justin. "So sorry. Something came up. Make it up to you sometime?"

I decided not to question the question mark at the end of his message. Was he going to make it up to me or not? No matter, because I had already moved on to the next course. Back at the hotel, I took a long hot shower, daydreaming all the while about Paul, who'd suggested I return to the restaurant "real soon."

# CHAPTER NINE

# I Went on a Date and I Didn't Miss You

Two nights later, I returned to the restaurant with my college friend Mary, who'd relocated to L.A. The place was packed, and Paul was tending bar. He was surrounded by women who either wanted a drink, Paul, or both.

"Are you really six two?" one of the women asked. Upon sight of me, he motioned us over to two empty seats at the end of the bar.

"You just made my night," he said, placing down two wine glasses and uncorking a bottle.

"I know," I replied.

"No, really," he said, apparently unaccustomed to an upfront woman such as myself.

"I know," I repeated, leaning toward him. Mary was

taken aback by my feisty demeanor, which she, too, was unaccustomed to. She remembered me as shy.

"This is the new me," I said, clinking glasses with Mary, whose eyebrows were still raised. We sat and chatted and sipped on free wine, all the while assessing Paul. The way he flung glasses around in his black button-down, he seemed confident, a master of his craft. There is something satisfying about watching a person doing something they're good at. In the same way that Matt Damon makes me feel safe when he's robotically hopping rooftops in the Bourne Trilogy, Paul made me feel assertive, because he was.

At some point during the evening, Paul and his older, slightly sleazy coworker were hunched over the bar as I recounted the details of winning the Miss Lez pageant. Mary nudged me with her knee to try to stop me, but I was too entertained to stop. Their reactions were so predictable that I felt like a puppetmaster tugging at the strings.

"Yes, there is a swimsuit competition." Their eyes grew wide. "But not all the contestants wear swimsuits, actually." They sighed, disappointed. "For example, I went out on stage dressed as David Hasselhoff." They tilted their heads, perplexed. "Then I tore off the costume and morphed into Carmen Electra." Their eyes widened again.

At closing time, Paul invited me to stay and hang out while he cleaned up. Mary headed home, giving me a covert thumbs-up on her way out the door. As Paul counted the cash from the register right there on the counter between us, I basked in the intimacy of his trust in me. *This is the stuff girlfriends do.* Then he beckoned me into the supply closet for a kiss. It was cramped in there. We struggled to keep our lips locked as we tripped over mops and buckets, knocking piles of neatly folded napkins off the shelves.

"I don't think you're in any shape to drive home," he said.

"And whose fault might that be?"

"Well, I'll make it up to you by giving you a ride."

"How thoughtful of you."

"To my house."

"How opportunistic of you."

I guess it was true what all my friends always said about L.A.—that everyone there wants something from you. But that was alright with me, because I wanted it, too.

He pulled out of the employee lot in a Jeep, my number-one choice in the middle school game MASH. I was in heaven, cruising down the 101, Ben Affleck at the wheel, the warm L.A. wind in my hair.

On the front porch of his house, my knees buckled at the sound of a dog barking behind the door.

"Don't worry, that's just Louie," he said.

Ever since I was a kid, I have had a disproportionate fear of dogs. Like, yes, it makes sense to get a little bit nervous when you see a Rottweiler walking down the street toward you with no owner in tow. But to climb your parents as if they were a jungle gym at the sound of a dog's collar jingling? That is problematic. My fear of dogs supposedly stems from when I was a baby. There is a story about me in my stroller outside a store and a big ferocious dog scaring me. I can't quite remember the details, but here is the elaborated version I told as a kid, when embarrassed in front of my friends: "A giant German shepherd lunged at my jugular, and my dad dove into its path to save me just in time." It's probably more like: I was sitting in my stroller and I was hungry. My dad went into the store to get a snack. I heard a dog bark and I forever associated the sound of a dog barking with the fear of starving to death.

Luckily, Louie was not a Rottweiler, but he was a substantially sized dog. I leaned over to let him sniff my hand and did my well-rehearsed act of pretending to be cool. *Okay, Elena, just breathe. Don't be afraid, because dogs can sense fear, and if he senses fear, that might set him off. Breathe.* Pet, pet. *Breathe.* He brushed up against my leg.

"Aw, he likes you. He doesn't do that to just anyone."

"Really?" I knew that the answer was "No, duh, not really," but I really did not care. Turned on by the rush of the Jeep ride and threat of an attack dog, I launched myself at Paul, grabbing him by the shoulder and turning him around to face me. We kissed with ferocity, groping each other, flinging clothes off with the same finesse with which he mixed a martini. We made an abrupt, rough landing on his bed, and

Paul reached over to his nightstand to retrieve a condom. As he was tearing it open with his teeth, he joked, "I hope these haven't expired. I think they're from when I was fifteen."

"Well, I see you haven't grown since then, so at least it will still fit!" I burst into hysterics. *Wahahaha! I am so funny!* It wasn't even true that it was small, actually. And I wasn't meaning to perpetuate the myth that size matters, thereby wounding his ego so deeply that he might never recover. It was simply a perfectly timed, cleverly phrased, irresistible joke. But he didn't laugh along. And then it really did get small.

"Ohhh," Paul grunted, dropping the condom onto the floor and rolling over to the other side of the bed to go to sleep. I guess there are some things you just don't joke about.

The next morning I awoke to the sound of a coffee grinder. Louie must have sensed I'd woken up, because he trotted into the room and put his cold wet nose on my arm.

"Good morning?" I said tentatively, hoping Paul had either forgotten about my comment or had forgiven me.

"Morning, sunshine. Coffee?"

"No err, yes please. No sugar, just milk."

I peeked around the doorway of the kitchen and gave him a little frown.

"Forgive me?"

"You know, Miss Lez, you're gonna want to pump up the man's ego when it's in your best interest. Here." He handed me a mug and gave me a playful light spank. "There's a great brunch place up the street. You can borrow a T-shirt. They're in my dresser."

At brunch we each ordered two different things, one savory, one sweet. We talked about everything from eighties actor crushes (Wil Wheaton/Alyssa Milano) to secret dreams (pursuing professional figure skating/playing Thor in the feature film). Afterward, we practically ran back to his house and gave it another go in his bedroom. I didn't crack any debilitating jokes, and everything went smoothly—wonderfully, in fact. Afterward, Paul was sleepy.

"Take a nap," I said. "I'll take Louie for a walk." I was willing to overcome my fear of dogs to impress Paul.

Outside, I was beaming in my sunglasses, dog leash in hand. I felt proud, walking Louie around the lake. Perhaps some people even recognized Louie as Paul's dog. *Lucky me!* After forty-five minutes, Louie looked tired, so I tied him to a telephone pole and popped inside a café. I kept an eye on him at all times, on tiptoe, in line for my lattes. The last thing I needed was to lose Louie. When I got back outside, two girls at a table were looking at me and whispering. They looked from Louie to me and back at Louie again. It occurred to me that I might not be the only girl walking Paul's dog.

On the way back to his house, I fretted and tried to let go of bad thoughts. *Just be in the moment, Elena.* Living in the present is not my forte, and neither is juggling two lattes and a dog leash. I held my head high, looking cool in my shades, and added an extra spring to my step. *I've got this.* I did my best to ignore some guys yelling something to me from a parking lot, but when they persisted, I looked over and they were pointing at my feet. The leash had wrapped twice around Louie and once around my ankle. I was seconds away from either taking a nosedive or decapitating the dog. I thanked them, twisted my way out of the web I'd created, and humbly plodded the few remaining blocks to Paul's house.

Paul awoke upon our arrival, gave me a kiss, and took his latte into the shower with him. Then I had an idea. I enticed Louie onto the couch through a series of kissy sounds, whistles, and the fake out of treats in my hand. *Come here, dammit.* I wanted Louie to lie with me on the couch so that Paul would emerge from the shower to an irresistible scene. Aw, look at my new little family, he'd think. Louie finally jumped up onto the couch and I spooned him. *This is just the cutest!* I waited, pleased with myself. I was sure to win both of their hearts. And then, out of nowhere, Louie turned to me and let out a terrifying growl, baring his razor-sharp fangs inches from my face. I hurled myself up over the back of the couch. My heart was pounding. It came out of nowhere, Louie's rage. My legs felt like Jell-O, so I shut myself in the den and crawled to the computer to check my email. Looking busy was almost as good as looking cute.

Paul and I spent nearly every night of the following week together. After work, I'd head over to the restaurant, where he'd serve me a pot of tea to sip on while he closed up. We'd head to his house afterward and he'd say things like, "If I accidentally got you pregnant, that wouldn't be the worst thing." And I'd say, "At our wedding, we'll play Ben Harper" (Paul's favorite musician). Louie and I got along great as long as I didn't try to cuddle with him on the couch. Paul confided in me, sharing all his childhood woes, and I listened while holding his hand. At the end of the week, I left for a four-day trip to visit a friend on Maui. Paul drove me to the airport, and when I was getting out of the car, Louie cried.

"Don't worry, you'll see her again," Paul said, patting Louie on the head and leaning over to kiss me.

Maui was a euphoric long weekend of learning to surf and leaving things everywhere. I was so in love with Paul, I forgot my carry-on luggage on the plane. My head was in the clouds. I called him twice during my trip, and each time we talked, you could practically see our smiles through the phone.

"You're a goner," my friend said when I hung up the phone.

"I know!"

WHEN I RETURNED to L.A., I couldn't wait to see Paul. I called him and his voice mail picked up. I was disappointed, but as I was leaving a message, he called me back on the other line.

"I just missed your call. Are you home yet?" He sounded

excited to see me, too. We chatted for a few minutes and then he had to leave for work. I was a little curious why he didn't ask me to stop by the restaurant, but I figured it was a given. And then my phone rang again. That must be him, I thought, calling to remind me to visit him. It was TJ.

"Aloha!"

"Jackass, when you are done gallivanting all over the country, you need to come home and explain yourself. I can't keep making excuses for you. You know I have no imagination."

"Excuses?"

"Every time someone asks where you've been, I break into a cold sweat."

"Tell them I'm at work on the West Coast. It's quite simple."

"Yeah, but someone told someone else that someone told them that they saw you with some guy somewhere."

"Some guy somewhere? That could have been anyone."

"Exactly. At the rate you're whoring it up."

"Listen, dumbass, I have a serious question for you. You know the waiter I told you about?"

"The one who was flirting with all the other girls at the bar?"

"Do you have to remind me of that? It's different with us."

"Go on."

"Well, I just got back to town after not seeing him for four days, and when we talked on the phone just now, he didn't suggest I come see him at work tonight. Is that weird?"

"Do not go there."

"Why not? He even called me right back after missing my call the first time around."

"Trust me. Just don't."

"Ugh. Whatever. Tell me what else is going on. Give me some gossip."

"Most of it's about you."

"All righty then. Well, I have to get ready to go see him at work."

"I wouldn't if I were you."

I was nervous walking into the restaurant to surprise Paul. TJ had planted a seed of doubt in me, but it wasn't enough to outweigh the confidence I had in Our Connection.

Paul smiled when he saw me. I walked over and gave him a hug.

"Did you cut your hair?" I asked, fluffing the front of it.

"No."

"Oh, well you look cuter for some reason. It must be because I missed you."

I sat at a table, and he brought over a pot of tea. I sipped it and watched as he sailed around the room, dropping off plates here and there, chatting with customers. Then he came over, pulled me up out of my seat, and led me into the area at the back of the bar. *Yes! Another supply closet make-out session!* He sat me down on an empty stool.

"Listen, I'm calling this off," he said. "While you were gone, I went on a date and I didn't miss you." I laughed.

"I'm sorry. Please don't be mad," he said. I laughed harder. He maintained a serious expression.

"You're kidding, right?" I asked, my laughter gradually shifting into short gasps for air.

"I wish I were. Please don't hate me."

"Are you serious?"

"I am. Don't be mad, okay?"

"Uh . . . I'm not mad . . . I'm, confused," I said, the shock of it hitting me.

"So am I," he said.

I sat there staring at him, almost laughing again. So am I? What does that even mean? The moment felt surreal, like when I was knocked in the head by a softball in middle school. Everything went quiet and peaceful for a few seconds, and then came the wave of searing pain. I slid off my stool, looked him in the eye, and said, "Okay." I shrugged my shoulders, smirked at him, and walked out of the restaurant, resisting every urge to look back. My feet felt heavy, like I was wading through mud. I calmly walked to my rental car, got the keys out of my bag, opened the door to the back seat (where the windows were tinted), sat down, shut the door, and sobbed. And then I called my mom. It was 4:00 a.m. her time.

"Honey, what happened? Are you okay?"

"I'm fine, M-m-mom, I p-promise," I strained to form words while hyperventilating. "B-b-but. Paul said he w-w-went on a date with s-someone else and he d-didn't miss meeeheeehheee."

"Okay, which one is Paul, dear?"

"Mommm! The waiterrrrrr!"

"Right, I'm sorry. It's late here. Or early." The last my mom had heard, I was planning my wedding with Paul. But I couldn't blame her for not keeping up. "Okay, honey. Breathe. God I hate men."

"Me, t-toooooooooo!" My mom sat on the other end of the phone for half an hour while I cried.

"Be careful driving, and call me when you get home, please."

"Okay, Mom. I m-miss you."

Then I called TJ, who was less consoling.

"Unless you're dying, call me back in six hours. There's a *Knight Rider* marathon on."

"I shouldn't have worn this shirt! I shouldn't have worn this shirt!" I forced the sentences out through more sobs.

"Uh oh. I told you not to go there."

"You're not helping!"

"Okay, tell me what happened." I could hear TJ rustling around on the other end of the phone, most likely sitting up in bed and piling up the pillows behind her. She was a good friend. I told her the story.

"He's a dick, and it's better you found out now rather than three years from now, when you have a kid together or something."

"I know, b-but wahhhhhhhh . . . "

"Listen. Delete his number from your phone right now. Never contact him again, do you hear me? And come home. I miss you."

"You do?"

"I do. Now tell me, which shirt did you wear?"

"I hate you."

"I'm going back to my show now. Hang in there and whatever you do, don't call him."

There was no reasoning with me. It didn't matter what my mom or TJ or Megan tried to tell me.

"You're better off without him."

"You deserve someone way better."

"Elena, he's an actor."

There is no capacity for logic in the brain of the broken-hearted, consumed by thoughts of What I Could Have Done Differently. We tear ourselves apart, dissecting every decision that led up to the unfortunate outcome. I shouldn't have worn that shirt. I shouldn't have called. I should have played harder to get. I should have worn my hair down. I should have worn my hair up. I should have worn my favorite jeans/dress/jacket/hat/lucky necklace/short skirt/booby shirt. And then we call in the troops.

"What now?" TJ said, answering on the first ring.

"Be honest. Do I look better without bangs?"

THE TRUTH IS, when you finally meet the right person, you can do everything wrong and you'll still end up together. Amy had done everything "wrong" on our first date. The sun was out, the windows were down, and we were both giddy driving to the café to have tea when a guy cut us off at an intersection. Amy leaned across me, stuck her arm out the window, flipped the guy off, and screamed, "Fuck youuuuuu!" while somehow still steering the car. I sat calmly and quietly in my passenger seat while she gathered herself and apologized for her outburst. Later, in the midst of a passionate conversation at the café, she stood up abruptly and said, "I should take off. I have to finish up some work for my class tomorrow." Then she put on her jacket, dropped some cash on the table, and ran out of the café, leaving me sitting there alone to wonder what the heck went wrong and how I was going to get home. Six months later, we were living together.

As I drifted off to sleep, I consoled myself by recalling bits of wisdom imparted by my surfing instructor, which I vowed to apply to my love life as well: "Always check out the surf break before you paddle out. Watch which way the current is going so you don't get swept away. And don't be afraid. When it feels right, you'll know." I held on to his words like a life preserver.

CHAPTER TEN

# Second Wind

I'd always fancied myself one of those brokenhearted women you'd find slouched in front of the TV, sobbing through *Steel Magnolias* while wolfing down an entire pizza. I mean, that's what I did for fun, so wouldn't I turn to my usual comforts in a time of need? Rather, I lost my appetite, reluctantly crunching on cornflakes and quinoa crackers that I forced down with tea. Food brought me no fulfillment. I ate to live, which for an Italian girl is not living at all.

I felt like I'd had the wind knocked out of me, like when I went through my Mary Lou Retton phase in third grade, attempting front flips in the living room, landing flat on my back gasping for air. So I decided to go for a walk at Runyon Canyon, the windiest place I could find.

Exercise has always been the least of my interests. But they say it's the best thing for you when all you want to do is remain in the fetal position with a milk shake and a bendy straw. How maddening. I pulled into the parking lot, propped my foot up on the back bumper, and tightened the laces on my sneakers in which I intended to walk, not run. I felt like an actor in a montage scene, heroically conquering her gloomy blues and reentering the harsh but beautiful world. In my imaginary movie, I was being cheered on. Armed with my iPod, Kleen Kanteen, and a travel pack of tissues, I headed for the jogging path. I crossed through the gate, ready to launch into my victory lap. *I can do this!* And then I stopped dead in my tracks. There were dogs everywhere.

Blasting Ben Harper from my headphones, I took a deep breath. And then a step. Then another. And another. I braved my way past the Yorkshire terriers and yellow labs. I took another deep breath. And another. Walking felt good. I considered changing the music. I knew Ben Harper was not the best soundtrack for my makeover montage, but I was taking baby steps. And then the tears returned. I walked and cried, shocked that there could possibly be more tears to shed, and walked and cried some more. Real actors sprinted past me in a waft of coconut-scented sunscreen and perfume. All the while, Ben crooned in the background: "When your whole world is shaken from all the risks we have taken."

I walked until I was dripping with sweat and tears. People stared at me like I was an alien. I probably looked like one. And suddenly I was crying from a different place, for all the little darts in my heart.

Age five: My classmate Tina didn't invite me to her Easter egg hunt.

Age eight: One day, out of the blue and outside of our YMCA after-school routine, my boyfriend, Warren, playfully pushed Vicki Amendoli around the gymnasium in the race car tire rather than me.

Age nine: A deep betrayal by a family friend. An arrow, not a dart.

Age eleven: During English class, my friend Missy wrote notes back and forth with the boy I liked. The notes, which I later retrieved from the garbage can of our empty classroom, said mean things like, "Elena should shave her mustache," in the graceful flowing script I recognized as my friend's. My heart crumpled like the paper I held in my shaking hands. I ran to the bathroom to inspect my trembling upper lip.

Age thirteen: Nonna Dina died.

Age sixteen: I drove four grueling hours to see a boy. Upon arrival, he kissed me and said, "Hey, I'm going to the skate park with my friends. Do you want to come and hang out, maybe read a book? There are some really nice benches there."

Age nineteen: The girl I didn't realize I was in love with moved across the country. I was devastated, but I didn't know why.

Age twenty-one: When I returned home from a trip out of town, I found out the girl I'd been dating had started seeing someone else. They came in together to visit me at the coffee shop where I worked. The new girl was supercool, an art school student. I served them lattes in my required uniform: a denim button-down shirt with the company logo over my heart.

Age twenty-four: The badass biker girl I'd been dating rejected me gently in her early morning whisper, "You're the perfect girl for me. I'm not ready for you."

Age twenty-nine: Amy and I broke up.

Age thirty-two: "I went on a date with someone else, and I didn't miss you."

And that was the short list. I'd been through stuff, bigger stuff. I'd been to the dark parts of myself. I'd worked my ass off to love me, and my dating frenzy was proving counterproductive.

To stop the inner dialogue, I decided to focus on my surroundings. This is one way of meditating, I'd been told, and the only kind I am capable of. I have no patience for sitting in a chair. I began walking again, noticing the crackle of wood chips beneath my feet, the scent of sagebrush in the breeze. The sun shone on the rocks, illuminating the various shades of brown, gray, and gold. The West Coast light is different, flatter. The trees cast sharp shadows on the cliffs—bigger, taller versions of themselves. It was a wonder how they persisted, their roots erupting from the parched ground. I looked down. The cracks in the dehydrated dirt formed tiny landscapes at my feet. Millions of minuscule canyons. A hawk hovered over a field. Joggers trotted past me. Life was happening. Walking was the only thing to do, and so I did. I walked and walked until I rounded a corner to a vast view of the city and the Pacific Ocean in the distance. My heart swelled in my chest.

I found a bench away from the bustle and sat down. I closed my eyes. The sun's warmth felt like love filling me up from the inside. I soaked it in for several minutes. When I opened my eyes, peeking out of the dirt in front of me was the hint of something shiny. I dug it out. It was an old key that had clearly been there for quite some time. There was no chain attached to it, no name. I sat holding it, amused and a little perplexed. It was warm in my hand. It felt like the key was there for me. And then, out of nowhere, I began to laugh. The laughter was hearty, emanating from a deep place. Joy had snuck up on me. I'd sat in that same place many times before, brokenhearted, disbelieving, mad at myself and the world. And no matter how shattered I'd ever felt, love always found a way of finding me. I laughed and laughed. *Look at me! I can open my heart, be vulnerable, act like a lunatic, and have my heart broken!* Isn't that what living is for?

It was suddenly clear that what I'd become attached to was not so much the waiter himself, but the idea of love. Sure, I'd fallen hard for him and the future I'd prematurely fantasized for us. But sobbing for days over someone I'd known for a mere week was an overreaction, even for me. I was in love with love. I always had been. I was never cut out for one-night stands, and though my enthusiasm might have scared the waiter away, I was not about to let that stop me. I would hold out for someone as eager as I was.

I scaled the steep steps back up to the parking lot, smiling and thinking, *Wow, these stairs really suck, but I'd do it all over again, gladly.*

A FEW DAYS later, I received a phone call from my mom.

"Hello?" I reached for my headset to safely talk while driving.

"Hi honey. Listen, your brother is fine, but—". I pulled over to the side of the road. My heart simultaneously leaped out of my chest and caved in on me. I burst into tears before she could even get a word in. "Elena, he's okay. But he's in the hospital."

My brother had nearly been hit by a car on his bicycle (my biggest fear nearly realized), and in the process of swerving out of the way, he had taken a fall so hard that he broke his hip. They were still conducting tests, but all looked okay otherwise. I sobbed by the side of the road. My little brother had the wind knocked out of him, too. And for real. It was time to go home.

CHAPTER ELEVEN

# Balance

**F**resh off a red-eye, I headed first to the grocery store and then to my brother's apartment. I perched on a stool in his kitchen while he relayed the details of the accident and his surgery. I whipped up oversized servings of our Sibling Special: cheddar, tomato, and avocado omelets. My brother's bum leg took up the entire couch, so I plopped myself down on the floor below him and balanced my plate on my knees. We ate in front of reruns of *The Office* and laughed at all our favorite parts. *Phew*. He was okay. I was okay. We were going to be okay.

I'D BEEN HOPING to touch base with Megan so I could invite myself over to her clean house to hang out. But she wasn't returning my calls, so I made my way to TJ's instead. It was always safer to keep my shoes on while navigating the maze of dirty socks and stray bits of cat poop at TJ's house. Her overweight cat, "Shrimp," didn't always have the best aim when using the litter box.

"Are these clean?" I examined a pair of sweatpants I found slung over a chair in her room.

"I have no idea what you're referring to," TJ shouted from the living room, "but the answer is no."

I slipped into the sweatpants, stole a bag of popcorn from the endless supply in her kitchen, and collapsed onto her couch. She grabbed a handful of popcorn from the bag on my lap, spilling half of it all over the place.

"Really?" I asked, already knowing the answer. "You can't just take one small handful at a time like a normal human being?"

TJ chomped away with a smirk on her face.

"I like to make sure there's enough in the cracks of the couch in case I get hungry later."

It was *Shark Week*. We watched episode after episode until sundown, at which point I dragged myself to the subway and made my way back to my brother's house.

The odds of being attacked by a shark are one in eight million. What are the odds of meeting that special single someone in a city of eight million?

I WORKED FROM my brother's apartment for a couple of weeks, until he was on his foot again (he had to keep pressure off the broken side for another month). Once he was able to hop around his apartment and complete such tasks as cooking, cleaning, and picking on me, it was time for me to go.

Between Megan seemingly avoiding me and my fear of facing Noah, I couldn't bear returning to the office. So I fled to the closest remote place I could think of: Martha's Vineyard. My college friend Alexis had grown up there, and I'd exhausted every excuse not to go. I'd always pictured Martha's Vineyard as an island of narrow streets overcrowded with Croc-clad yuppies from Connecticut, where I grew up. The bars would surely be packed with guys wearing Black Dog T-shirts and shorts with whales on them. Martha's Vineyard was so not me. It was the perfect place to hide.

When you live in New York City, your perspective is a little skewed. I know that "the Vineyard," as the regulars call it, is not nearly as remote as the middle of Maine, but for true New Yorkers, anything north of Massachusetts might as well be Canada. The Vineyard felt far from civilization because it proved impossible to get to. It takes six hours no matter which way you slice it, and forget about trying to book a weekend ferry during the peak summer season. Luckily, with my boss's recent move to California, I was still able to work "from home." I booked a Wednesday afternoon boat.

As I stuffed my bathing suit and flip-flops into my bag, I caught my reflection in the mirror above my dresser. I looked lost, and not like on the TV show of the same name, on which they are all tan and toned. I was pale. And tired. Below the mirror was a photo of my grandmother, which I took into my hands. In the picture, she is in her fifties. She's already had her kids and her divorce, and she emanates a feminine authority that I've always aimed to possess. The face in the mirror across from me displayed hints of her essence—some of the strength I'd inherited; some attained on my own. The rest I had yet to earn. I placed the picture down and picked up a deck of cards I kept next to two of her thimbles: gifts to me upon her death. The cards were hers, too, and when I was young we'd play our favorite Italian game together. Though it was a game of chance, I still attempted to cheat once, organizing the cards so that all the high cards were lined up for my picks. She smacked my hand and said, "Cheating takes the fun out of it." Then, in the same stern tone that made me feel safe in the world, "You'll never know what fate had in store for you."

"It's in your hands now, Nonna," I whispered, blindly choosing two cards from the deck. "You pick for me." A five and nine of diamonds.

"I have no idea what that means," I said. I finished packing and left the two cards faceup on my dresser.

It was midweek, so I got a much coveted table all to myself on the ferry. An episode of *Top Chef* was playing on the TV above the snack stand. As fate would have it, the very first woman I'd ever dated was a contestant. She lashed out at her teammates with the same venomous Scorpio wit that had won me over at nineteen, when she had betrayed her brash exterior and held the door for me. I took the sight of her as a sign that life is a series of cycles, more of a circle than a straight line.

When the ferry pulled into Vineyard Haven, I jumped out of my seat and ran to the edge of the deck. All the buildings in the storybook town were of the same country style, with the same cedar siding that over time fades to dolphin gray. Upon disembarking, I drove by a sign for the Black Dog Café and decided to stop in for a glimpse. I'm not going to lie. The place is cute. I passed the day working there and then made my way up-island to meet Alexis, who was tending bar at her parents' inn. The drive itself was rejuvenating. The trees, so lush and green, created a canopy over the road, opening up now and then to offer a picturesque view. The Vineyard actually did look like the oil paintings I'd seen in town earlier that day: white sailboats sprinkled across a shimmering turquoise bay; a field of deer, heads down, fluffy white tails at full mast; a hillside farm, its red barn blazing in the setting sun.

Alexis's parents greeted me with hearty handshakes and showed me to my room. I instantly felt like family. The year-rounders differ greatly from the summer weekend onslaught. They are openhearted, hardworking, sunburned people of the earth. They cook and clean and dig in the dirt. I overheard talk of bonfires and skunk taming, whatever that was. I traded my boots for flip-flops and hung up all the dresses I would clearly not be wearing. I was ready to move in.

As she served up oysters and glasses of sauvignon blanc, I brought Alexis up to speed on my most recent antics.

"No way! Superscandalous!" she said, shining a glass and hooking it onto the beam above the bar.

"I know, I know."

"But totally fun, too. Oh, and I know the perfect guy for you. My cousin Banyan."

"Banyan? As in Banyan Banyan?"

"Yes, you are totally his type. Hippie girl with long brown hair."

"But I'm trying to take a break here. That's the whole point."

"He's playing a show on Saturday. We'll go and I'll introduce you."

Banyan, the son of famous musicians, was hot and had a Vineyard house all to himself. It had been only half a day, but I was already dreading the boat ride back home. There's something especially calming about islands, knowing there is a moat separating us from all the things we need to do. The overflowing laundry pile back home would just have to wait, as would the countless phone calls yet to return. I never thought I'd be grateful for shoddy cell phone service. There was a sea in between my concerns and me, and Banyan was my ticket to paradise.

That night I fell asleep to the image of my life as a year-rounder. I couldn't wait to spend the rest of my days riding horses and sipping herbal iced tea by the pool.

The following day, my mom came to join me for some mother-daughter quality time—meaning by day we'd hang out at the beach and at night I'd ditch her to go out with Alexis and her friends. I picked her up at the ferry dock in my new Crocs. They're so comfortable! On the way back up-island, we stopped for ice cream at the famed Mad Martha's. As we strolled along Main Street, racing to catch the runaway drips of mint chip in the sweltering sun, we perused the window displays of framed cliff-side sunsets, straw hats, and pastel linen dresses. And there, crossing the street, was Banyan.

"Oh my God, Mom, don't look! That's Alexis's cousin, the one she wants to set me up with."

"Where?"

"Don't look!"

I turned the corner and pulled my mom with me. My heart was pounding.

"Did you see him?" I asked, panting.

"You told me not to look!"

I turned to find myself face to face with a life-size poster of him, advertising his upcoming concert.

"That's him!" I said, pointing at the poster. His dreamy smile sent me adrift. *I could work at his mom's chic clothing store in town and get a family discount!*

"Hmm," my mom said, crunching on her cone, "I don't see it." My mom often had psychic moments. That was not the moment for one of them.

"Mom! Don't put that out into the universe! You're ruining everything!" I screeched, stomping around like an over-tired six-year-old.

"I'm sorry, honey."

"That's it, end of conversation," I said, flailing around and racing up the street toward the car.

I'd had enough of dating. I was ready to find a real, true love (or to marry for money, whichever came first).

That night over dinner at the inn, the topic of my future folksinger husband came up again.

"I'm sorry honey, but I just don't see it," my mom said.

"I don't care what you see or don't see, Mom, just stop saying it out loud. You're jinxing it," I said in the calmest voice I could feign in my state of rage.

And then . . .

"I don't know," she said, gazing off into the distance as if suddenly spotting a pirate ship sailing toward shore, "I just had this vision of you falling for some guy who works in a kitchen."

I glared at my mom and gulped down the last of my wine. When we'd both destroyed our dessert, I tucked her in for the night and headed down to the bar to see Alexis. She was polishing the last of the wine glasses. I grabbed a napkin and helped her.

"You ready for another Vineyard adventure?" she asked. "We're going into town, to Back Door Donuts. They sell fresh donuts out the back door at midnight. Hence the name."

"Are you kidding me? I just ate a five-course meal," I said, holding my stomach.

"Go get your shoes on."

"Will Banyan be there?"

"You never know. It's a small island."

"I'll be right back."

Five of us piled into Alexis's '85 Land Cruiser and headed down-island toward town.

"Alexis, why is it called down-island," I asked, "if we are actually traveling north?"

"It's related to which way the wind blows."

"Don't forget we have to pick up Day Time on the way," one of the cooks said from the back seat.

"Who's Day Time?" I asked.

"You haven't met Theo?" Alexis asked, seeming surprised. "He's the daytime cook. As fate would have it, the nighttime cook is named Theo, too. So they're Day Time and Night Time to us."

"Nope, never met him," I said.

We pulled into Theo's driveway and out bounced this young, energetic guy in a Mets cap and old-school Nike high-tops. He took his hat off and twisted his wild mess of brown hair into a soccer player bun. He had (almost) the build of a soccer player, too. At about five foot ten, he was well pro-portioned; toned with just enough padding to make for good cuddle material.

"Hey-yo! Whoa, there are a lot of us. We can take my car instead," he said, swinging his keys around and heading toward a white Caravan.

"Ha! Nice car, Day Time *Dad,*" I chirped.

"Uh, Alexis, who is this? Making fun of my car already. It's a little far to walk from here, you know."

"This is Elena, my friend from New York," Alexis said, linking her arm in mine.

"Oh, you're from New York?" he asked.

"Well, I grew up in Connecticut, but I've lived in Brook-lyn for—"

"Ohhh, Connecticut," he teased, and closed the driver-side door before I could finish. I slid open the back door and fell into the van, littered with damp beach towels and magazines.

"Wow. Are there seat belts back here or what?" I asked, digging around the cracks of the seat for a buckle.

"There should be."

"Oh yes, here it is, right underneath this Justin Bieber CD." I waved it around for everyone to see before handing it to him.

"That's my cousin's."

"That's what I would say, too," I replied.

"Wow. I like you!" he said.

"I like you, too!" I exclaimed, meaning it.

We drove down to the donut place, a caravan full of cooks and waiters singing along to Led Zeppelin.

"Did I see a pool at your place?" Alexis asked Theo as we wound our way toward town.

"Yep."

"No way. We are so going back there later tonight. Will your family mind if we take a midnight dip?"

"They'll be sleeping. We'll just have to keep quiet."

At the donut shop, Theo offered me a bite of his apple strudel.

"No thanks," I said, not wanting to offend him. "But it does look delicious."

"Come on," he said, holding it under my nose. The scent of freshly baked apples was tempting. "It's so good."

"No, really. But thanks."

The third time he offered me a bite, I said, "Look, I'm allergic to apples. And nuts. You're basically trying to kill me."

"Well that's not going to work. All apples or just cooked apples? All nuts? Maybe it has something to do with trees. Tree fruits and tree nuts?"

I'd been warned that my thirtieth birthday would be a turning point, after which it would take me three days, not one, to recover from a night out. As the year had unfolded, that had turned out to be true. In addition, I was introduced to new creaky aches and pains and the mysterious emergence of allergies.

"Nah, I'm just getting old," I said, smiling.

"Let's go to Balance," Alexis said, tossing her sticky cruller wrapper in the trash.

Balance was a bar close to the ferry dock in the center of town. It was a bit of a tourist trap, but on the Vineyard, the year-rounders all know one another, so Alexis greeted the bartender, and those of us who weren't driving were offered beers on the house. I scanned the bar for Banyan. He would have stood out at six foot four, but he was nowhere to be found. I'd primped for nothing. Back at the inn, I'd changed into my favorite shirt for the outing, just in case. In the midst of the rowdy crowd, Theo emitted an essence of calm. He was the eye of the storm. It was in the way he stood so confidently, comfortable in his body. And it was the way he made me laugh. I wanted to be near him.

Over songs by Oasis and Coldplay, Theo and I shouted to each other about food, New York City, and climbing trees as kids.

"One time," I said, leaning in closer to his ear, "I climbed a tree in our front yard. It was a pine tree, just like tons of trees I'd climbed before. I made it to the top and then almost back down again. But when I reached the lowest branch, I froze. It wasn't even that far from the ground, but for some reason I got scared and yelled to my mom, who was somewhere inside the house. 'Mom, Mom!' It took several shouts before she came running outside, my little brother in tow. They started laughing at the sight of me hanging helplessly from the branch with only a four-foot drop below.

"'Elena, what's wrong? Just let go. You're close to the ground,' they said. I couldn't let go. Eventually, my mom came over and helped me down. I was ten at the time, and we'd recently watched *Challenger* explode on takeoff. I had learned that we don't live forever. We would all die; not right then, but someday. And that kept me clinging."

"My grandmother was diagnosed with cancer when I was five," Theo said. "And we moved from Nicaragua, where my mom is from, to New York to be with her. My family was very open about it, explaining to me that she was sick and that she was going to die soon. It didn't scare me. I was sad, of course, but I understood that it was a natural part of life. People tend to underestimate kids. I remember the last time I saw her. No one told me it would be the last time, but I knew. I wanted to tell her I was going to miss her, but I was too shy to say it. And then she died. But even at age five, I knew that she knew. You know what I mean?"

"I do."

Then he flashed me a huge smile that I returned, suddenly dizzy. I headed to the ladies' room to collect myself. While waiting in line for my turn, I realized I was still smiling.

Along with Alexis and another cook, Sal, we left the bar

and headed back to Theo's house for a swim. We pulled into the driveway with the headlights off, so as not to wake one of his nine family members up from Manhattan for the weekend.

"Poolside," Theo whispered, returning from the dark garage with an armful of towels. The four of us tiptoed down the wooded trail, trying our best not to snap any loud twigs. Sal, who'd had one too many beers at the bar, got snagged on some prickers and uttered a stifled, "Shit!" We all bounded down the rest of the trail suppressing hysterics.

Theo playfully flipped the sign on the pool door from WELCOME to BEWARE. Below the letters was an illustration of a group of women swimming in the buff. He explained that his great-grandmother had made the sign for her afternoon women-only skinny-dipping tea parties. Cool family, I thought.

"Okay, turn around and don't peek," I said, slipping out of my jeans. Theo turned around to face the opposite direction, but Sal slumped in the lawn chair, staring blankly through me. You couldn't see much by the light of the moon anyway. In honor of Theo's great-grandmother, I tossed off my shirt and dove into the deep end. Theo joined me shortly after, doing a half dive, half cannonball in his boxers. The pool was cold, so Sal and Alexis refused to join and instead witnessed our underwater races from their seats. Theo grabbed my toes when I was winning, and we both resurfaced laughing and choking on chlorine.

And that was it. No kiss. No groping underwater in the dark. Just a ton of fun. When I pulled myself out of the pool, I felt lighter than I had in a while, even as I shivered under the weight of my cold, wet hair.

I got dressed, gave Theo and Sal (who had passed out) a hug goodnight, and left with Alexis.

"That was so much fun. Theo is a really cool guy," I said.

"Theo is awesome. A better match for you than my cousin, actually."

"No, no. I don't mean like that. He's just—"

Then Alexis pulled over to the side of the road abruptly and turned off the headlights of the car.

"Look! An owl. See it up there on the telephone wire？" she asked, pointing.

"Where？ I don't—oh! Wow, how did you see that？" Its white chest was barely visible against the night sky.

"I love owls. I can spot them a mile away," Alexis said.

We sat and watched the owl for several minutes. As my vision adjusted to the dark, I could make out its head turning from side to side, looking around, most likely for food. We are all on a search for something.

# CHAPTER TWELVE

# Fireflies

In the morning, it dawned on me that I'd forgotten my phone by Theo's pool. On my way to join my mom for breakfast, I signaled to him from outside the kitchen window. When he stepped out onto the porch, his eyes, the color, how they sparkled in the sunlight—I nearly fell backward off the porch at the sight of them. During the prior evening's outing, it was too dark to notice his eyes, their blue-green hue that precisely matched the Atlantic as seen from the cliffs up the street from the inn. I found it hard to form a sentence.

"I, I think you may have my phone," I stammered. Theo stared back at me with the same stunned expression I must have had. At his side was Pedro, the son of one of the employees, a precocious seven-year-old who followed Theo everywhere, the two of them speaking a mélange of Spanish and Portuguese, their common mother tongues.

"Oh. Well, um, why don't you come back to the kitchen at seven when I get off work, and we'll go and get it together?"

"Okay."

Pedro stood there staring up at us with an expression that said, "What the heck is wrong with you guys?" Then he handed Theo the ring from a game where the goal is to swing it on its rope and have it catch on a hook on the opposite wall. Theo tried it once, missed, and ran back inside. Pedro looked at me, shrugged, and handed me the ring.

After my breakfast of pancakes minus the blueberries, a custom order to piss off the kitchen staff, my mom and I walked down the steep cliff-side trail to the beach. There were very few people, save the random solitary elder nude male sunbather. The seagulls performed nosedives, impressing us with their consistent catches. The sandpipers did their sprints alongside the shore, leaving a trail of the tiniest footprints to be washed away by the waves. It was a perfect day. My mom and I were getting along great. In general, we get along really well, but there is always the possibility that I can become annoyed with her for no reason whatsoever. I think that's pretty normal, but I was grateful for a day where it didn't even bother me when she stopped to meditate on a big slab of driftwood.

"Go ahead, Mom. I'll be over here hunting for shark's teeth."

Following another hour or so on the beach, a few hours of work, and one bike ferry ride to The Bite for its famed fried clams, it was finally time to meet Theo. My mom trekked up to the lighthouse to catch the sunset, and I went to fetch him from the kitchen.

"Want to follow me in your car?" He asked. "Once I get the van home, someone's bound to steal it, and you'll be stranded there along with your phone."

"Sure," I said, giddy at the thought of being stranded with him.

As we pulled into the driveway, I could see into the kitchen through the bay window at the front of the house. His entire family was sitting down to dinner.

"You coming or what?" Theo asked, walking toward the door.

"Yep."

Sure enough, all nine family members were assembled around a giant dark wood farm table, and every single one of them looked up when we entered the room.

"Hey guys," Theo said. "This is Elena."

"Please, join us!" his aunt said, sliding her chair over a few inches, making room for me.

"Thanks, but we've got plans," Theo said, saving me. *We do?* Theo knelt down to greet his nephew, who was eating Cheerios off the tray of his high chair.

"Did anyone find a phone out at the pool?" Theo asked. I had forgotten all about my phone. I was too busy imagining what our kids would look like.

"Yes, along with a pair of socks," his twelve-year-old cousin said, getting up to retrieve the goods from a shelf above the fireplace.

"Those aren't mine," I said defensively, feeling self-conscious. "They must be Sal's."

Once outside, I asked the best possible question for courting a chef.

"Are you hungry?"

"Always," Theo said, breaking into a big smile.

I drove us to town, to a spot Theo had heard of.

"They say the burgers are good."

"Say no more."

Then something odd happened. We drove in complete silence for ten whole minutes, and it wasn't odd at all. There's a lot to be said for that. When two people can enjoy the sweetness of no sound, not needing to fill the space with words, it can feel more intimate than talking. The sky turned pink and then purple as we wove through hillsides dotted with cows and sheep. Now and then, on a hill high enough, we could spot the ocean in the distance.

"Want to split a burger?" I asked, perusing the menu.

"Sure, and a couple of apps?"

"Perfect." Not everyone will split food with me, which is my preferred way to order. It's not that I want less of my meal. It's that I want some of everything else, too.

Theo ordered generously, opting for the mussels and

risotto cakes to start, and to follow, the burger cooked medium-rare, my favorite. Once we both had some food in us, we picked up where we'd left off the night before, discussing our shared experience of growing up with two cultures. Though his mom is Nicaraguan and my dad is Italian, there were many similarities. We were both sent to school with lunches made up of things no one had ever seen before. Theo's rice and beans weren't as valuable a trade as my Nutella sandwiches. It was one of those conversations where I had to force myself to stop talking and take a breath to take a bite of my burger. It takes a very compelling distraction to keep me from my food.

"I saw a sign for ice cream at the mini-golf place we passed on the way here," I said.

Theo snatched up the bill. I dove toward it to no success.

"Okay, I'll let you pay," I surrendered, "but only if you let me treat you to a round of mini-golf."

"If you really want to end this nice night by having your ass whipped."

"Listen, buddy, I grew up in the suburbs. I'm quite skilled in mini-golf, bowling, and *Street Fighter II*."

We made it to mini-golf just in time for one round. The teenage summer staff didn't even give us attitude for showing up right before closing time. It was proceeding to be a perfect day.

"I wonder if they have our favorite flavors," Theo said, squinting in the floodlight at the ice cream menu. "They do!

We'll have a large cup, please. Half cookie dough and half mint chocolate chip."

We took our ice cream and golf clubs to the first hole. I took a bite of ice cream, set my pink ball down, and gave it a whack with just enough force to get it over the hump but not out of the green felt course. We laughed our way from the windmill to the dinosaur, Theo teasing me at every putt. Mini-golf reminds me of middle school, as did the way he made me feel. I could have been thirty or thirteen, though I was grateful for the self-assurance that comes with age. At thirteen, I didn't know where to put my arms, the way they dangled, so long and lanky, seemingly out of proportion with the rest of my body. With Theo, I joked and pranced around, feet planted firmly on the ground, my arms leading the way. And I was winning.

We continued to exchange snapshots of our childhoods. My Connecticut upbringing was predictably comprised of sequined jazz dancing, horseback riding lessons, and a BMX bike obsession, thanks to the movie *Rad.* Theo, having spent the first five years of his life in Nicaragua, had some more unusual anecdotes.

"We played baseball with a sock wrapped in tape and made slingshots from strips of old tires."

"What did you shoot at?" I asked, taking a swing and sending my ball sailing through the metal loop in the middle of the course and out the other end, nearly making a hole in one.

"Anything that moved." Theo lined up at the tee.

"Did you ever get anything?"

"Of course."

"Then shouldn't your aim be a little better?" I teased, waving my club at his golf ball.

"I'm accustomed to moving targets. Why don't you go do a little jazz dance over there, and we'll see how I do."

One of the fifteen-year-old staff members from the mini-golf office came over to have us pay up, since they were closing soon. I whipped out my wallet first and paid the bill in full.

"Keep the change," I said, feeling deliriously generous.

"Really?"

I later realized I'd given the kid a 100 percent tip. I had lost my mind.

If we hadn't been rushed through the rest of the course, we might have kissed in the plastic cave, the way we lingered in there. My hands were shaking as I struggled to align my golf club just so, torn between winning and tapping my ball into the water so we could stay in there forever. The self-assured woman had flown the coop. I pulled the sleeves of my sweatshirt over my clenched fists.

"I let you win," Theo said when we tallied the score.

We pulled out of the parking lot and headed back toward Theo's house, where I would drop him off, bringing our impromptu date to an end. Again, the silence. I drove slower than I normally would, shifting gears now and then.

When I did so, my hand would brush against his knee. He didn't move out of the way.

"That's the turn for my house," Theo said as we passed his road. "If that's where we're headed."

I zoomed past it. A few minutes farther up the road, when my headlights bounced off a reflective sphere, the only marker to the entrance to my favorite stargazing spot, I abruptly swerved onto a dirt road. The parking lot was technically off-limits, accessible to permit holders only. But at night nobody bothered to patrol it. The cops were too busy pulling over teenagers on their way home from the bars. We had the whole place to ourselves. Theo got out of the car first and went to sit on the rocks overlooking the moonlit ocean. I was suddenly shy, as happens with people I really like, and that was how I knew I did. I wound my summer scarf around my neck and saddled up next to him.

"Look," he said, pointing out to the ocean.

"What?" I asked. As far as I could tell, all that spread out before us was a pitch-black sea.

"Look again."

I sat up and squinted. As each wave crashed, it was illuminated from the inside.

"Whoa. What is that?"

"Bioluminescence."

My inner marine biologist lurched back to life.

"It looks like a billion fireflies!"

I'd learned about bioluminescence during freshman year marine biology and had stored the memory of it as a source of inspiration on rough days. If those crazy-looking creatures could light up in the darkest of places, the little light in me could stay aglow in the face of the most dreadful of times. I vowed to someday scuba dive the Great Barrier Reef to witness bioluminescence for myself. And suddenly, there it was, off the coast of Massachusetts. Sometimes the thing we're looking for is right there in front of us. We just have to adjust the focus.

"My grandfather is a minister," Theo said. "He says that people are like fireflies. If we choose to come together to work toward peace, we can shine as brightly as lanterns, light-houses even."

We zoned out for awhile on the wonder of the living lights. I swaddled myself in my hoodie, my makeshift cocoon. It wasn't the same comfortable silence we'd experienced in the car to and from our date. It was the kind that twisted my nerves into knots. I was afraid I might hurl my dinner over the edge of the cliff. I could feel him looking at me now and then, and I knew that if I met his gaze, we would kiss. I was terrified, which was odd considering all my recent flopping around with guys like the fish out of water that I was. So why couldn't I kiss Theo?

By the summer between eighth grade and high school, all my friends had already kissed guys, so I had to get a move on. Brandon Edwards and I had a daytime date at the movie theater in town. I had my mom drop me off down the street and out of sight—it was embarrassing enough that I wasn't allowed on dates at night. Brandon was skateboarding with a few other freshmen-to-be. The boys flaunted their first few sprouts of facial hair, shaped into would-be goatees, and I was looking pretty cool in my matching mint green shirt and socks from The Gap.

"See ya, guys!" Brandon yelled to his friends over the sound of skateboard wheels screeching on the forbidden strip mall sidewalks. He glided toward me and skidded to a halt, tapping the back edge of his board to pop it up into his hand.

"Hi."

"Hi."

A sticker flashed across the back, bold red print on a white background: SKATEBOARDING IS NOT A CRIME. Was it a crime to go to the movies during the day as an excuse to hang out in the dark?

"Well, honey, you were kind of on a mission," my mom said later that evening as I stomped around the house.

As much as I loved Winona Ryder at the time, I'd barely caught one scene of *Great Balls of Fire!* during my date with Brandon. We were too busy kissing in the back row. When we weren't kissing, I was distracted, the big screen a blur before me. All I could think was, *I just had my first kiss. I just had my first kiss!* I couldn't wait to tell my friends. But Brandon beat me to it.

Even before cell phones, the rumor spread across town like the Nutella I layered on my bread to console myself. Brandon, upon rejoining his friends outside the movie theater, relayed the details of our date. Apparently, his version was: "She attacked me."

"I attacked him?" I flailed the knife around in our country kitchen, dipping in for more and more chocolate hazelnut therapy. My mom listened from a safe distance on the opposite side of the island. It was true that I had placed my hand on his knee one minute into the previews, but I didn't tell my mom that. It was also true that I had approached the date the way parents shopped for Cabbage Patch Kids in the eighties, when mob mentality led to casualties at stores where the highly sought after dolls were selling out. I was leaving that date with my first kiss, and I was taking no prisoners. I simply couldn't start high school without it. But I certainly wouldn't be making the first move again anytime soon.

I had been making the first move left and right with all the recent guys, and none of them had turned out so well. Maybe men preferred to be the one in control, to play the knight sweeping in and . . .

I shook my head. *What the? I don't actually think those things. I'm a feminist. Anyway, he would probably be totally psyched if I—*

And then he kissed me. He leaned in toward me, I turned to face him, and he kissed me. I was thirteen again. Only this time it was a nighttime date, and nothing else existed.

We swiftly moved to the back seat of my car, where it was warmer, and spent an hour hugging, kissing, and grasping on to each other with the fervor of having just met a missing part of yourself. I couldn't get close enough to him.

"Why don't you come back to my tent with me?" he asked, tracing the outline of my eyebrow.

"Your tent?"

"Yes, my entire family is here for the weekend, as you recall, and all the beds are taken. I'm out in the back yard in a tent. You're tired, and it's not safe to drive all the way back up to the inn at this hour."

"Umm, no," I said, imagining the morning walk of shame past a buzzing house in the interrogating morning sun.

"Come on, the tent is far from the house. No one will even know you're there. And we'll cuddle up just like this and sleep."

"No way," I repeated, crawling up to the driver's seat. "As much as I'd like to."

"Don't worry, I'll behave myself, I swear."

"It's not you I'm worried about," I said, pushing in the clutch and starting the engine.

At the end of his driveway, Theo hopped out and trotted around the car to my open window for one last kiss.

"See you tomorrow," I said.

"Is it tomorrow yet?"

I drove away slowly, letting the dreamy air of the evening linger along the winding uphill journey back to the inn.

# CHAPTER THIRTEEN

# If You Want a Nice Catfish, Order the Grouper

"That's him, I know it," my mom said.

"Huh?" I looked up to see Theo gliding across the lawn in his clogs, carrying a tray. There was a tail hanging off one end. When he saw us, he swiveled on his heel to head in our direction. As he got closer, the scales on the striped bass glimmered in the sunlight. My stomach did a backflip. Theo looked handsome in his chef jacket. And he could fillet a fish. Pedro, as usual, trailed behind.

"Mom, this is Theo," I said, after attempting to give him a hug that just turned out to be awkward, what with the giant fish in the way and all. My heart was racing.

"Hi Mom!" he replied emphatically. We all exchanged curious glances, not excluding Pedro. *Hi Mom?* "Hey, I'll call you later when I'm done," Theo continued, nodding toward me nervously. "Nice to meet you!" And he scurried off toward the kitchen. For Theo's every step, Pedro took two to keep up with him.

"Can I say it now?" Up in the room, my mom wrapped her new wind chime in a towel and wedged it into her suitcase.

"Say what?" I tossed her the shampoo bottle she'd forgotten in the shower. She placed it in a plastic bag and slid it into a side pocket of her suitcase. And with that, she zipped it up and whirled it around to the floor in one swift motion, pleased with herself.

"That I was right? If I'm not mistaken, isn't Theo some guy who works in a kitchen?" She flashed me a side glance.

"Mom, we had a fun time, that's all," I said, failing to convince even myself. A smile crept up and out of me.

At the ferry landing, the last of the passengers whisked past us on their way up the ramp onto the boat. I hugged my mom goodbye one last time.

"Don't do anything I wouldn't do!" She turned to join the herd. We both knew I'd done a million of those things already, but she liked to say it anyway. My parents met each other at eighteen when my dad was sent over from Italy to the United States for a work exchange. Early into his internship, my mom's long legs caught his eye as she ascended the steps of the office entrance, and his white kneesocks won her over at the company softball game. (He wore them with a suit.) They fell fast and madly, but soon his visa was up and he was forced to return to Italy. They wrote impassioned letters back and forth, but their longing wouldn't tolerate the distance. A few months later, my mom had a plane ticket in her hand.

"Clarice, you may as well pack up your desk, because you know you're not coming back," her coworkers teased.

"Don't be ridiculous. Of course I am." My mom left her framed photos and coffee mug on her desk just as they were. At the airport in Milan, she was overwhelmed, surrounded by sniffing Doberman pinschers and *carabinieri* with machine guns. She didn't speak a word of Italian. And to top it off, my dad wasn't there to meet her.

"I'm so stupid," she said to herself, sobbing on the bench surrounded by families embracing. "He's Italian. He probably has fifteen girlfriends." And then she looked up and there he was, running toward her with a bouquet of flowers.

"That very moment, I knew I wasn't going back," my mom says whenever she tells the story. It's no wonder I'm a hopeless romantic at heart.

Alexis had the morning free, so we took her twins to the beach. They dug for crabs in the red sand while we sipped on smoothies and caught up on girl talk.

"Why didn't you go back to his tent with him? Tents are so romantic!"

"Maybe in high school. Or on a honeymoon in Greece," I said, reaching around to apply sunscreen to the back of my neck.

"Girl, do you realize what you've done?" Alexis said, fanning the air with her magazine.

"What?"

"All my friends here are desperate to meet someone, and you come along and scoop up the one single great guy on the island."

"I know. He's pretty perfect, huh?"

"Honestly, I can't think of one bad thing about him," Alexis said.

"Yeah, he's pretty amazing. How old is he, though? I can't tell."

"He's twenty-five, I think. Yeah, twenty-five."

"What?" I closed my magazine and looked at Alexis. "Oh no. No no no."

"What's wrong? You're the older woman. It's hot. Very Demi Moore."

"When I was sixteen, he was eight. No no no. I've had enough trouble with guys my age. The last thing I need is a younger man."

"Oh come on."

"Are we still going to Banyan's show tomorrow?"

"Yes, but . . . "

I tossed my *Us Weekly* onto my towel and got up to join the girls in the sand.

I avoided the inn all day. At seven o'clock, Theo called. I knew he had just gotten off work. I stared at my phone, frozen. *This guy is different*, I told myself. *He's mature.* But I'd been through so many bizarre experiences with men, I didn't even know if I trusted myself anymore. I pressed "ignore" and let him leave a message, which I listened to immediately.

"Hey Elena, it's Theo. Just got off work and wondering what you're up to. Give me a call."

I took the low road and texted him back.

"Hey, tonight's girls' night out, but have fun whatever you're up to." I cringed as I wrote it. It was such a cop-out, such an obvious diss. I cringed. *What the hell is wrong with me?* Send.

"Okay, well let me know what you're up to after." Theo's reply was direct, seemingly unaffected by my mock nonchalance.

Later, at a kitschy little Mexican bar in town, I clinked margarita glasses with the girls. With each sip, I blurred a little bit more the memory of how much I liked Theo. He was so wonderful, but so young, and I wanted things like a home and a family. He was twenty-five and living in a tent. With the added help of Alexis's friends egging me on, by the end of the evening I was back on the Banyan bandwagon.

"Girl, Banyan is so hot. I think every woman on this island would kill to be in your shoes."

"Hey, if you hook up with him, that means we'll be invited to his parties. His bandmates are pretty luscious, too."

"You could join him on his tours and see the world!"

"Alexis, why didn't you ever set me up with him?"

"We're invited to the wedding, right?"

Alexis remained quiet. She was willing to humor me by taking me to Banyan's concert, but of the setup, she was no longer a fan.

I didn't write Theo back that night. The following day he called again. Normally this type of persistence would turn me off, but his assertiveness impressed me.

"Hey lady, it's Theo." His tone was cheerful. "I hope you had fun with the girls last night. There's a bonfire tonight at Philbin. Let me know if you want to come. We can pick you up on the way down from the inn. It's a little hard to find in the dark."

I texted back: "Hey Theo, I'm going to see Alexis's cousin play tonight, but maybe we'll come by afterward." That was a lie.

Up in my hotel room, I was extra careful brushing my hair because there was some woman in the room down the hall who had just gotten a brush so stuck in her hair that they had to cut it out. Her fiancé to be was downstairs at the bar, waiting to surprise her with a proposal. I put on one of the dresses that had been gathering dust and wondered if the woman got the brush stuck on purpose.

"Listen," Alexis said when I met up with her to leave. "I've got to get back home after the concert because the girls aren't feeling well, so we should take two separate cars. But don't worry. I'll introduce you to Banyan, and you can go to the after-party."

"You're not coming with me?" I scowled.

"You'll be fine!"

I followed Alexis as she pulled into the parking lot of The Hangar. She drove us right to the front of the building and into a space marked PERSONNEL ONLY. I'd grown accustomed to her rebellious island ways. The Vineyard laws were apparently open to interpretation, and every other cop was her cousin. She pointed at the space next to her. Reluctantly, I took it.

"Come on, I think he started already," she said, grabbing my hand and dragging me to the entrance.

It seemed like the entire island was packed into the place, and every single straight woman was in the front row. Alexis grabbed my hand, and I trailed behind her to the back of the bar, where her brother and some friends were standing. They sang along to all of Banyan's songs while I brainstormed names for our kids. He was gorgeous—tall, toned, and tan— and with that guitar slung around his neck, I was a goner. I wouldn't even mind when he went on tour. I'd stay home and hold down the four-thousand-square-foot fort. No problem.

After the concert, Alexis pulled me backstage. Banyan was in a room with his bandmates, and she waltzed me right up to him.

"Hey cuz, what's up?" She hugged him. "This is my friend Elena. She's visiting from New York."

We shook hands, and Alexis whispered something to him. She stayed for another ten minutes and then left to go home. I made friends with the bass player. We chatted while Banyan addressed his adoring fans. Then he came back into the room.

"We need some rides back to the house. Does anyone have space?"

"I do," I said.

"Cool. You guys go with Elena, and I'll be there soon."

I ended up driving the bass player and two random guys to Banyan's house. We pulled through the gated entrance and made our way up the long winding gravel driveway. When we passed the horse barns, I suppressed a squeal. We took the fork in the road that led to his house, and I imagined myself taking that turn many more times in my future. I'd have a trunk full of organic groceries, including cases of goddess dressing and fresh veggies from the farm stand up the road. Then I would get home and cook up some brown rice in my oversize rice cooker, which would fit in our kitchen because it would be so big, bigger than New York kitchens. *There would be so much space! We could have house parties and invite people from the neighborhood!*

We got out of the car and walked up to the front door, which was unlocked because it's Martha's Vineyard. Yep, the kitchen was definitely big enough for a twelve-serving rice cooker. And it had skylights! *I could hang lots of plants from the ceiling. I could make macramé plant holders like my mom used to make in the seventies. I could bake pies and cookies and learn how to make croissants. I could do yoga in the living room.* My fantasies unfolded with each turn of each corner of the six-bedroom, five-bath house. And then Banyan showed up. With a girl. And they were holding hands.

"Hi, I'm Vespa," she said, reaching out her hand. Great. I'd already been burned by a Vespa, and now I had to forfeit my future husband for one. As it turned out, it was a sweet surrender, because she was so extraordinarily likable (and pretty) that I was kind of crushed out on her myself.

"I'm Elena. Nice to meet you."

I decided to stay at the party in case there might be another guy for me, one of Banyan's friends, perhaps. Double-date horseback rides with Banyan and Vespa! The British piano player and I took turns deejaying on the iPod while a bunch of girls danced around the dining room. When I tired of that, I joined some others around a campfire in the front yard. We sang along to classic rock songs, to which Banyan strummed the melodies upon request. And so the night wore on. I chatted with this person and that, sat around, danced a little, and ate up every snack in sight. That's always the best part of parties: the food. At some ungodly hour way past my bedtime, I wandered out to the barn, where I stumbled upon the guys taking shirtless turns on the Pilates machine. They were flexing, showing off for each other, grunting and pulling this weight here, stretching that leg there. So that's what guys do in the locker room at the yoga studio. One of Banyan's friends walked over to me.

"So, tell me again what it is you do in New York." I hadn't told him, but I dismissed that minor detail.

"Well, for my day job, I work in finance." At this, his eyes glazed over. "But I love to write and dance and—" It was too late. I'd lost him. He was zoning out on his friends playing Ping-Pong across the room. I watched the little white ball float back and forth across the table. Ping pong ping pong. *What am I doing here?* I missed Theo, who listened.

Having turned down several offers to share a bed with a persistent guitarist, I crashed on a couch in the living room.

When I awoke a few hours later to a headache reminiscent of my rave days, the sun was up. And so were the guys. They hadn't gone to sleep yet and were still drinking beer. The very thought of it made me gag. I heard someone say the word *pool,* and I dragged myself sloth-style across the floor in hopes that water might make me feel human again. *This isn't worth the pony.* I fetched my bathing suit from my car and followed the train of fumbling zombies up the path toward the pool. And that's when I met my ex-future mother-in-law. Banyan's famous folksinger mom was standing at the top of the path in the most beautiful silk dress. She was backlit, and the sun created a halo effect, just like on an album cover. I squinted. Yep, it was really her.

"You guys look pretty ragged," she said as we approached. "You should come in for some toast." She turned to walk inside.

We followed her into her delightfully decorated, hippie-inspired, immaculate house. I ate my toast over my plate so as not to drop a single crumb on the floor. And then I had to pee. I admired the baby pictures on the wall in the hallway on the way to the bathroom. *Our kids would have been so cute. Oh well.* And then I did what I always do at the most inconvenient, inappropriate time. I clogged the toilet. I have this terrible habit of using way too much toilet paper, and I'd been spoiled by the robust prewar plumbing of New York City. You could flush a television down the toilet at my Brooklyn apartment but not, as it turns out, on the Vineyard. After wrestling with the plunger for five minutes, I reentered the kitchen and hugged everyone goodbye.

I got into the driver's seat of my car and tossed my flip-flops on the passenger-side floor. My mom hates it when I drive barefoot, but I love the feeling of the cool pedals on my feet. It makes me feel free. I sat behind the wheel, wondering where to go. The answer was obvious, but my own game of ping-pong was still in full swing. *He's young. But so sweet. He's young. But so smart. He's young. But so insightful. He's young. But so funny.* It was Sunday, so I knew he didn't have to work. Hands trembling, I texted him.

"Picnic at the beach?"

My phone chimed less than a minute later. "Sounds like a plan."

On my way to fetch Theo, I stopped by the overpriced market for provisions. I put special care into choosing. I'd never fed a chef before. The clerk rang up my hummus, heirloom tomatoes, baby carrots, multigrain baguette, chocolate, and my splurge item, $8 lavender goat cheese. Theo was cleaning a window screen in the driveway when I arrived. He walked over to me with a wide smile and his confident stride. My shoulders softened at the sight of him.

"Hey lady!" He gave me a kiss. It felt natural to greet him like this. "Come in for a sec and meet my little sister. She's leaving for college next week."

Little sister? I panicked and reached around to the back seat. I grabbed my most accessible layer: a black zip-up hoodie from the Lexington Club, a San Francisco lesbian bar. It was eighty degrees out, but last night's low-cut dress was not quite family appropriate. Theo held my hand as we walked up to the house. On the front porch, he flung open the screen door, stepped aside, and placed his hand on my lower back, letting me in. And so I met his sister, looking like a nutcase in a sweatshirt in the middle of summer (not to mention the illustration of the topless tattooed babe on the back). His sister was adorable; a younger, female version of Theo with more freckles. She shook my hand warmly.

I let Theo drive us down to the beach, though he'd never

driven a stick shift before. He stalled several times but didn't grind the gears once. *This could work.* He parked, and we kissed in the car before getting out to wade across the shallow channel to the beach. The water was waist high, rushing past us and out into a saltwater pond that eventually met up with the sea. Rowboats with names like *Littleton, Whitehurst,* and *Finn* carved into them lined the shore.

"Can't we just take one of these?" I asked, reluctant to wade across. Swimming in Theo's pool at midnight was one thing. Wading through a muddy pond in a bikini in broad daylight was another.

"No such luck."

I waited until he had walked past me before I kicked off my flip-flops and pulled off my dress. Of course, he paused to let me by.

"Ladies first."

The current was strong enough to keep me focused and therefore less self-conscious, but not strong enough to carry me away. I focused on the trail at the other side of the pond that would lead us up and over the dunes. Theo carried the towels, and I struggled to suspend the picnic bag above water. The water was getting deeper and deeper. Suddenly, a ruckus sent a ripple our way. A loon had landed.

"Hey lady, don't let that good-looking bread get soggy."

"Don't make me laugh and I won't," I said, picking up the pace to distance myself from him.

We strolled along the beach in search of the perfect spot. Walking beside him, a feeling of familiarity washed over me, like we'd been walking side by side all along.

"How about up there by the dunes?"

"Perfect."

We each grabbed one end of my old dorm days tapestry and laid it down on the warm sand. I opened the bag of carrots, then the hummus, cheese, and bread.

"These don't really exist, you know," Theo said, picking up a baby carrot.

"What do you mean?"

"They're just big carrots that they cut down to this size."

"For real?" I examined my carrot.

"I'm afraid so."

And we ate. A carrot dipped in hummus. A bite of bread and some cheese. Some bread, some cheese, and some hummus. When a bug landed on my side of the blanket, in full-on city girl fashion, I shrieked. Theo flicked it off, and it landed on its back in the sand. Distressed, its little legs flailed to find the ground. Theo got up, walked over, bent down, and coaxed the tiny insect onto its feet. When it finally flipped over, it flapped its wings a few times and flew away. I was soaring, too, on the possibility that Theo might also treat me with such tenderness. We lazed around on the beach blanket, eating, laughing, and kissing for hours.

"I'm sorry I didn't call you back for a couple of days," I

said, drawing a circle in the sand with a twig. "I got freaked out about our age difference at first, but then I decided to get over it, and I have."

"Good."

I got up to walk to the water, and Theo grabbed onto my ankle and scanned me from head to toe. I squirmed, feeling exposed standing there in my bikini. And then he said, "Mmm, I didn't know a woman could have so many curves." I ran the rest of the way to the water. *God, I love this man!*

Later, on the way back to the car, he stopped me by the path to the parking lot.

"You know," he said, sifting through the top layer of sand with his foot, "the strangest thought crossed my mind as I watched you take the food out of the grocery bag."

"Yeah?"

He was silent for a moment, and when I looked back at him he smiled, shook his head, and said, "I thought: I want this woman to feed my kids."

"I don't think so!" I kicked some sand at his feet and continued toward the parking lot. Then I turned around and said, "You're the cook. You'll be feeding the kids."

That evening we met up with the rest of the kitchen staff at Sal's house for a trash can clambake. While Theo and the other cooks tossed everything from seaweed to corn to beer into the pot, I had a moment to catch up with Alexis.

"It's funny," she said, observing Theo. "I knew him and

I knew you and I adore you both. But the two of you together never crossed my mind until I saw you side by side. Now it makes perfect sense."

When the clams were cooked, we all scooped heaping portions onto paper plates and sat cross-legged on the patio. Theo was the last to sit, having helped serve everyone else. He sat down next to me, his knee touching mine.

"Hey, Theo," Sal said, mouth full, taking a swig of his beer. "Didn't you guys do clambakes at that place you worked at in Maine? How was the food there?"

"Well," Theo said, swallowing. "Let's just say if you want a nice catfish, order the grouper."

Everyone burst into laughter. Alexis hunched over in hysterics. I didn't get the joke; cook humor, I guessed. People continued snorting and chortling. I already knew that Theo made me laugh, but apparently he made everyone else laugh, too. Theo, seeing my confusion, explained that restaurants are often caught serving up more readily accessible fish in place of what's on the menu. I smiled to myself and continued to chew. You don't always get what you order.

# CHAPTER FOURTEEN

# Five and Nine of Diamonds

I prolonged my trip in order to spend another three days with Theo, transferring from the fancy inn to a little duck-themed bed-and-breakfast nearby; less scandalous and less pricey. Everything, down to the toothbrush holder, had ducks on it. The sheets, towels, curtains, accent pillows, area rug, doorknob: ducks. From the balcony, we could see ducks in the yard below. The ring tone on the phone was *quack quack quack*.

"Hello?"

"Hey it's me. I just got off work."

"I'm hungry."

"Well it just so happens I'm holding a bag of food for you."

Theo and I spent every possible moment in my room. We ate and slept, and didn't sleep, and in the morning we pressed "snooze" on the duck alarm clock, spooning through countless nine-minute increments of bliss. We were well behaved at first, spending most of our time talking. Following my string of one-night stands, it felt nice to take it slow and get to know one another one anecdote at a time. That lasted thirty-six hours.

When I had to leave the Vineyard, I went kicking and screaming. But I had to get back home and tie up some loose ends. Like work, for example, which I'd neglected for days, remotely working my remote job. On the morning of my departure date, Theo didn't make it any easier to leave. He drove me over to his house, where he made me huevos rancheros from scratch. I marveled from my stool as he chopped tomatillos and onions into minuscule cubes for the salsa. I savored every bite of my breakfast and nearly missed my ferry for all the smooches we snuck in down to the last minute. Had there been one more red light on my way, I would not have made my boat.

Once on the road back to New York, my phone service returned, and I called Megan. I left another message. *New Yorkers never answer their phone,* I told myself, trying not to imagine reasons she might be mad at me. TJ, forever Jersey at heart, picked up on the first ring.

"Dammit, you're alive?" she said, sounding out of breath. "I was hoping to inherit your apartment."

"Sorry, that goes to my brother. But I'll leave you my tea collection. Hey, I'm on my way back to the city. Entertain me. This drive takes forever."

"I would, but I'm on my way to meet up with a girl."

"A girl? But it's only 5:00 p.m."

"Yeah, well we're meeting up for a walk through the park first. Her idea. Then we're going to some new vegetarian restaurant in the Slope."

"The park? You? Then dinner? That sounds like a date. Are you feeling okay?"

"In fact, no I'm not. I've changed outfits twice. What's wrong with me? I think I turned into you while you were gone."

"Either that or you're whipped. Who is she?"

"You don't know her. We met at bingo night. I should have been going out without you a long time ago. I think you were cramping my style. So, white T-shirt or shirt and tie? Either way I'm wearing my leather jacket."

"It's a zillion degrees out. Don't wear the jacket."

"But we're taking my bike."

"She agreed to get on that thing?"

"She's already been on it six times."

"Six times? How many dates have you been on? It's only been ten days. You are such a lesbian."

"Whatever, asshole. T-shirt or tie?"

"Tie. Wow. I think your news is more shocking than mine," I said.

"What's your news? You knocked up? I coulda told you that would happen."

"No, jackass. But I did meet a guy. A funny one. Even funnier than you."

"Impossible. Look, I'd love to continue with this chitchat, but I gotta go meet Antonella."

"Antonella? An Italian girl. I always knew you were in love with me."

"This is the sound of me hanging up on you."

I FELL SWIFTLY back into my New York routine, trotting up and down the subway station stairs and weaving my way around tourists. All the while, I had my phone in hand, texting my friends and pretending to myself that I wasn't waiting for Theo to call. I knew he worked crazy hours and had limited cell phone service on the island, so for the most part I remained calm by focusing on the memories of our time spent together. But when, on the fourth day, I finally called and he didn't pick up, I did what any sane, grown person would do. I deleted his number from my phone.

My mind went wild with possible scenarios. Maybe he met someone else. Maybe he lost his phone. Maybe something happened at work. Maybe the island is under water. Maybe he realized I think too much. Maybe he thinks I'm too old. And then the phone rang and it was him. I jumped when I heard his custom tone, the xylophone melody that sounds like something profound is bound to happen.

"Hello?"

"Hey lady! You're on the ferry on your way to see me, right?"

"I wish," I said, putting my phone on speaker so I could continue tearing open the plastic bags on the counter before me. "Actually, my friend Megan is about to get here. We're ordering in from my favorite Thai place."

"I'm jealous. More of the food than of spending time with you."

"Of course. I really miss Mad Martha's mint chip. How's the Vineyard treating you?"

"It was better when you were here."

"I was trying not to worry when I hadn't heard from you," I said, trying to sound nonchalant.

"Oh, sorry babe. Things have been nuts at work all week. And you called while the Jets game was on. They won!" Right. Football. I hadn't thought of that.

"Hey, will you be home later?" I asked. "I really wish I could talk to you right now, but I can call you back when Megan leaves."

"I should be around. Call me on the landline," he said. "And hey."

"Yeah?"

"I miss you."

"I miss you, too."

I dumped the food from the takeout containers onto plates, my pumpkin curry looking much more appealing than Megan's gooey yuzu stew. I don't like my food slippery. I portioned out the cucumber salad and opened the dipping sauce for the order of dumplings to share. Megan buzzed my door at precisely eight o'clock. She was always prompt, like me. We hugged in the doorway, a little tighter than usual. Megan flipped her shoes off and started talking before she even sat down.

"Oh my God, girl, I missed you. I'm sorry I went MIA, it's just, there was something I had to do, and I had to do it on my own."

"What are you talking about?"

"Jared. I know you hate him, and that if I asked your opinion—"

"*Hate* is a strong word," I said. "It's true that I've never thought he deserves you, but the heart has a mind of its own. Trust me, I know. So I'm sorry if I—"

"I quit."

"You did?"

"Yep. And I told him where he can stick his iPhone."

"Yes!" I gave her a high five. "Phew, because I really do hate him." We sat down in front of our feast.

"Yeah. I had really lost myself there. I don't know what I was thinking."

"You weren't."

"I got obsessed with wanting him to want me, and I didn't stop to realize that I don't really want him."

"We all do it."

"And you know what the worst part is? He tried to turn me against you. When I told him I didn't want to waste my time with him anymore, he said that you were planting your feminist ideas in my head. Amazing, right?"

"Ah yes, me and my outlandish ideas, like that women should be treated with respect. Cheers to unreasonable standards!"

"Ha! Cheers to that!" *Clink.*

We ate and talked, all the while reaching over each other for another dumpling or helping of curry.

"Then he finally broke down," Megan continued, "when he realized I was really calling it off. He told me he loved me, but he still didn't offer to commit to me. Instead he nearly started crying, saying, 'I'm so fucked up,' and all this bullshit, which normally I'd fall for." She took an assertive sip of her Thai iced tea from a straw. "The old me would have sat down next to him on the bed, placed my hand on his back, and listened. But instead I was like, 'Yes, yes you are,' and I grabbed my bag and walked out without looking back. I was kind of shocked, like, *Is this me?* It felt so incredible. I guess something in me had finally had enough, because some other force took over."

"You go girl. And I hear you. Theo is so nice, which, in the past, might have been a turnoff for me. But I'm old enough now to find kindness attractive. It's about time. It's kind of like you said, something in me had had enough. I'd reached a point where I was like, *Really? This is what's out there?* It was alarming. I was about done with dating. It didn't matter whether I found myself with a woman or a man in the end. I just wanted to be with someone kind and warm and ready, and dating sometimes makes that feel less and less likely. And then Theo came along."

When we'd polished off every last bite, we went to get ice cream, all the while crossing our fingers that my computer would continue downloading the movie I chose for us to watch.

"Oh my gosh, Theo would love this!" I said, picking up a new Ben & Jerry's flavor: Half Baked. "Chocolate chip cookie dough is his favorite."

"I know, you said that already."

"I did?"

"Yes, at the part about the mini-golf date."

"Oh right. God, I really am smitten, aren't I?"

"You sound a little like me with Jared. Are you sure this guy's as great as he seems? I mean, you don't have the best gauge, Miss Lez."

"I know, I know. But trust me, I'm sure."

"Well, I'm just checking, because you have a little bit of that possessed thing, when you first meet someone and all you can do is think about them."

"That's not true!"

We brought our ice cream home, grabbed two spoons, and plopped down on the couch to watch *Ratatouille*.

"This is the movie you picked?" Megan asked, clearly displeased.

"It's good, trust me!"

"Wait, you've already seen it? Let me guess, with your new girlfriend, Theo?"

"What?"

"You are such a lesbian. Let me guess, you're moving in together."

"Whatever. Just pass me the ice cream."

When Megan left, I called Theo back and we talked until 3:00 a.m. I fell asleep curled up under the covers like I did back in middle school, when I'd sneak phone calls past my bedtime. The following morning, my cheeks were sore from smiling.

"I'M HERE, DUMBASS."

"Be right down!" I ran out into the hallway, called the elevator, rummaged through my bag for my keys, ran back into my apartment for my lipstick, locked the door behind me, and dove into the elevator just as the doors threatened to close. Gwen Stefani serenaded me on my way down to the lobby: "If I could escape and re-create a place that's my own world." Mine was the only residential elevator I knew of that played music, theme songs for the movie of my life.

"Come on, we're late." TJ flicked the back of my head.

"And whose fault is that?" I went in for the attack hug,

wrapping my arms around her, pinning her arms to her side. "I missed you!"

"Get off me with your sperm germs." TJ pushed me away and then pulled me back toward her, resting her arm too heavily on my shoulder.

"Ow."

TJ, not short on subway fare but forever a rebel, jumped the turnstile.

"I'm nervous," I said as we boarded the train.

"Dude, chill out. The MTA police aren't going to arrest you by association."

"No, dumb ass. I'm nervous about seeing people at the party." We were headed to the birthday barbecue of one of our friends.

"You're old news, Miss Lez. Cheryl just got a part on *The L Word,* so everyone's all excited about that. And hey, when you meet Antonella, talk about how tough I am, okay?"

On the patio of the Cattyshack, I took my time dressing my tofu pup in every condiment on the table, dreading the one question I couldn't answer myself: Why a guy? My friend Erica bumped elbows with mine and reached across me for the ketchup.

"Hey, Miss Lez, where have you been? We've missed you. I hear your new boyfriend's a chef. When's he going to cook for us?"

How did she know about Theo already? I emitted a nervous giggle.

"As soon as he's sure it won't be him on the spit," I joked.

As the night rolled on, we gossiped, played beer pong, and made s'mores on the grill. To my relief, no one was grilling me. It felt good to be back on familiar turf. Then one of my butch friends, Hillary, came over and sat sidesaddle across my lap. She knocked back the rest of her beer. Her weight, all muscle leaning into me, made it difficult to breathe.

"So, Miss Lez, what do you think of my new grill? It's a ForeMAN."

I looked up at her. TJ spit some beer onto the patio. My distraught expression prompted Hillary to modify her tone. She shifted on my lap, softening from confrontational to playful. "Well," she said, handing me a beer, "mine's top of the line. Fully loaded." And then she winked at me. "Cheers." We clinked bottles and she got up to throw more charcoal on the grill.

Later, as the sun was setting, I was watching women cuddle up together and counting the water tower silhouettes on distant rooftops when I was hit with the New York Feeling. It happens now and then, and it comes on suddenly and strong. The beauty of the city, in all its complexity, combined with the realization that I live there, takes my breath away. This time was followed by a wave of nostalgia, for which I was no match. I sensed a cry coming on. I locked myself in the bathroom. A few minutes passed before there was a knock on the door.

"Just a sec."

"It's me, jackass."

I opened the door. Upon sight of my tears, TJ sighed and shut the door behind her.

"Look, I didn't tell them about your sexcapades. They must have heard from somewhere else. Word travels faster than your nose is running right now. Here." She handed me a wad of toilet paper.

"It's not that," I said, blowing my nose. "I don't even know why I'm crying." I rolled up another wad of toilet paper and blew my nose some more. "I miss this."

"This?"

"This." I waved my arm around the graffiti-plastered bathroom. "I miss the feeling of a room full of women. I miss the flirtation. I miss line dancing night. And bingo. And the cuties with their tattoos. I miss you. But I miss Theo, too. You'd really like him. He makes fun of me like you do."

"You hated line dancing! And anyway, I'm right here. And this Theo character sounds pretty good. Look, we both know I'm no expert in matters of the heart, but I'm pretty sure you can't control where it leads you. And wherever it takes you is where you end up. So what if you end up with a guy? It doesn't mean you can't still come to this bar, or go line dancing if you really want to. Isn't happiness the end goal, no matter what it looks like? Isn't that the whole point of all this?" TJ mimicked me, waving her arm around the bathroom like I had. "Besides, no one really cares as much as you think they do. The only person judging you is you." TJ stopped, stunned. "Did I really just say that?"

"Did you read *Eat, Pray, Love*?" I laughed and cleaned up my smeared eyeliner with a wet paper towel.

"Yes. I stole it from your house, and I read it on a meditation retreat in Tibet. Now let's get back out there before people think we're hooking up in here. I don't want to be tainted along with you." TJ gave me a pat on the shoulder and left me alone to fix my hair.

When I returned to the party, the guest of honor was opening her gifts. Women were huddled around her. TJ waved me over to where she was sitting.

"Dumb ass, this is Antonella."

"Oh, do I have stories for you," I said, shaking hands with TJ's new girlfriend. I took a seat next to them.

"Do you guys want anything? I'm going to fetch some cookies," Antonella said, getting up.

"I love her already," I said. "I'll take three."

"How 'bout you, babe?" Antonella stroked the top of TJ's head, eyeing her lovingly.

"Nah, I'm good." TJ tried to suppress a smirk and gave Antonella a smack on the ass as she walked away.

"Someone seems happy."

"How could she not be? She's with me." TJ leaned forward, resting her elbows on her knees.

"I mean you, idiot."

"Who me?" TJ smiled and looked at the ground. "Well, I hate to admit this over a girl, but yeah, I'm pretty damn pleased." Then she looked at me and flexed her arm. "You know, in a tough kinda way."

There was an uproar in the gift opening corner.

*Woop, woop!*

One of the women had unwrapped a dildo and was waving it above her head. Hillary, who was scraping the char off the barbecue, turned to face me.

"I'd say that's a pretty realistic-looking one. How 'bout you, Miss Lez?" Suddenly all eyes were on me. I glanced at it, took a sip of my beer, and shook my head in disagreement.

"No. It's bigger than average."


AS I WAS packing my bag to go back up to the Vineyard to visit Theo, I noticed the cards I had left out on my dresser while packing the first time around. I had forgotten I'd placed my fate in Nonna Dina's hands. The cards were dusty, and as I brushed them off, I gasped. A five and nine of diamonds. I dropped the T-shirt I had in my hand. A five and nine of diamonds. Theo was born in May, the fifth month, and I in September, the ninth.

"Nonna Dina," I said aloud, accusingly, amused. I picked up her photo. Of course she would choose a chef for me. She lived for food. I take after her in that way.

Theo was still at work when my ferry pulled in, so I went directly to his house. I was looking forward to showering, slipping into my sexy pajamas, and tucking myself into bed with a good read to wait up for him. However, the five cars in his driveway left me guessing I would not be donning silk anytime soon. The beat of the Black Eyed Peas song became more and more audible as I made my way up the path to the front door. Great. The house had been taken over by ten of Theo's twentysomething friends.

"Hi." No one even noticed when I entered the kitchen. I placed my bag down and grabbed a glass of water. Then I called Alexis, who was just closing up the bar.

"Hey, it's me. I'm here at Theo's house."

"Awesome. We're just about done cleaning up, and then we're headed over there. Your man's got a little party planned."

"I noticed."

I freshened up in the bathroom and then took a seat at the table, trying to be cool with the situation at hand.

"Elena, you want in?"

"In on what?"

"Round of poker."

"Oh, I don't really know how to play. I've only done the slot machines, but thanks." Then I thought for a minute. I really wanted to be more laid back, more adaptable, more fun. "Actually, I'm in." I grabbed a beer from the fridge. *I can do this.*

Alexis arrived forty minutes later, along with another close friend of ours from college.

"Alexis! Jane!" I jumped up and hugged them in the doorway. "Save me!" Alexis looked around and asked, "Where's Theo? He's not here yet?"

"No."

"Oh, I thought he left before us. He must be getting beer."

"Guess so."

And then the door swung open and Theo walked in and scooped me up into a big hug.

"Hey lady!"

"Hey."

"What's up, guys?" Theo went to high-five his friends and then announced, "Bonfire at the beach!" We slowly made our way out of the house and down to the beach. I did my best to be enthusiastic. *A little romance around the fire under the stars. Perhaps someone has a guitar. Theo and I could snuggle up under the blanket. It might be nice even.* And then it started to rain.

"Elena," Alexis said, getting up from the log we'd all just settled down onto. "Get your shoes." I grabbed my shoes and chased after Alexis and Jane, who were already at the car. Theo was walking toward us with a bag of ice.

"Hey babe, where are you going?"

"To my house," Alexis said. I opened the back door of her car and got in. Theo ran up to the window. I rolled it down and he gave me a kiss. We were so different; different ages, different desires, different species almost. He wanted to party and I wanted to read books in bed. But there was a current so strong when our lips came together that for a second I doubted my decision to leave. But it was raining and cold. And I'm old.

"Have a nice time with the girls tonight, babe. Promise you'll come cuddle up in the morning?"

"I promise." I kissed Theo one more time, and Alexis put the car in reverse.

Falling asleep on the couch at her house, I didn't feel vindicated. I felt hollow. I hugged the pillows into my chest to try to fill the emptiness.

The following morning, I awoke to the scent of fresh coffee and the sound of a dog barking. From the bay window, I could see Alexis and the twins walking down to the chicken coop for some eggs. I got up to make tea. Theo would be expecting me, hoping even in his sleep to feel me sneak in and join him under the covers. I knew that, and I felt like a jerk for leaving. But I was still upset. I glanced at the clock. My back was sore from sleeping on the couch. Alexis and the girls returned with buckets of eggs.

"Lena, look how many eggs I got!"

"I got even more. Look at my basket, Lena!"

Jane and her husband came downstairs, followed by Alexis's husband, who makes the best home fries ever. We ate a huge breakfast of the freshest possible scrambled eggs, free-range bacon, greens from the garden, and just the right balance of crispy to moist home fries. The food was delicious, and the clock was ticking. The more time went by, the more I felt the weight of what I'd done. It wasn't necessarily a huge deal that I'd left Theo to his party with his friends. It was more my own party inside that worried me. I had lashed out at Theo in a fit of fear, and it was taking everything in me not to shut down and shut him out. I knew myself. At the slightest hint of rejection, I was prone to donning the jet pack and fleeing the scene. But I didn't want to sabotage what we had, because deep down I knew that Theo did not mean to hurt me. So instead I washed the dishes and had Alexis drive me to his house.

"If you need me, just call and I'll come pick you up," she offered, pulling into the driveway.

"I think it's going to be fine. Thanks, girl."

There were bodies everywhere, people passed out on top of each other, and empty beer bottles all over the kitchen counter. I stepped over arms and legs, making my way to his door. A bolt of fear flashed before me. *What if he's in there with someone else?* I turned the knob on the door slowly. I peeked my head into the room, and there was Theo, alone in the middle of the bed, sleeping. I closed the door behind me, tossed off my shoes, and crawled in next to him, scooting up into the nook between his shoulder and his neck.

"Baby, hi. What time is it?"

"Don't worry about that," I said, and kissed my favorite spot under his eye, where his cheek meets his nose.

"Come on, let's go down to the beach," I said, tugging him out of bed.

"Okay, okay," he said, pulling on his khakis.

"I'll meet you outside."

We walked along the shore, leaving his friends behind to stew in their sweat. There was no one else on the beach and therefore no sound other than the occasional seagull and the crashing waves. And then the tears snuck up on me. I was doing pretty well while I was distracted. But I have no defense in the face of the sea. Its power to wash truth to the surface should never be underestimated. When I lived in San Francisco, I would sometimes go down to Ocean Beach just to hear myself think. It always worked and usually resulted in tears of varying kinds. Sometimes they were tears of fatigue, often tears of gratitude. This time, on the beach with Theo, they were the type of tears I couldn't define. They just slid freely from my eyes, the silent kind.

"You're quiet," Theo said, stopping to examine a horse-shoe crab shell.

Then the flood came. *Wahhhhh!*

Poor Theo was taken off guard. He looked as spooked as the deer I had nearly hit on my way up to the inn one night.

"Baby, what's wrong?" He turned to face me and pulled me into a hug.

"I don't know," I said. And I should have left it at that, because I really didn't. But I just had to go and put words to it, and they came out all wrong.

"You didn't even seem to care that I brought you bagels from Brooklyn," I blubbered into his T-shirt. "And your bathroom is dirty."

Theo was quiet for a moment. We sat down on a log, and I cried some more.

"I feel like you're attacking me," he said softly. "And I don't really understand why." His tone was tender, and I suddenly wished I could take it all back.

"I'm sorry," I said. "I don't even care about your bathroom. I don't know why I said that."

"Maybe you're just upset because you expected us to have alone time together?" Theo offered.

"Yes." *Sniff sniff.*

"I'm sorry, babe. I was thinking that last night, too. But I was just so psyched for all my friends to meet you."

"I know," I said, feeling lighter, understood.

"Anyway, we are having alone time now. Shouldn't we be enjoying it?"

"I suppose," I sighed, smiling ever so slightly.

I hate it when other people are right. Like my mom, for example, who said I'd fall for some guy in the kitchen.

"And hey," he said, nudging my knee. "You promised to come cuddle in the morning. And you showed up at noon."

"I know. I'm sorry," I said. "But I was too busy being upset because I wanted to spend time with you."

"That makes a lot of sense."

"Well, I never promised to always make sense," I said.

Theo pulled me in closer to him and squeezed me tight. "I don't expect you to, babe. You're a woman."

"Hey!" He already knew how to push my buttons. So I pushed him back, and he fell off the log. He pulled me down with him, and we stayed there laughing, looking up at the sky and getting sand in our hair.

# CHAPTER FIFTEEN

# Ratatouille

Theo surprised me one day. I was in the lobby of my apartment building, retrieving my mail as I did every evening upon returning home from work. On my way down the hallway toward the elevator, I was separating the L.L. Bean catalogs from my bills, wondering what I'd do about dinner. When I looked up to call the elevator, there standing in front of me was Theo.

"What⸮!" I dropped all my mail and ran into his arms. He had no choice but to succumb to my bear hug as I stood squeezing him and laughing hysterically. I love surprises. And I loved him. In that moment that much was clear to me. Taken off guard, without all my protective layers, defense strategies, and theories about love and life, and women versus men, all that mattered was that I lit up inside at the sight of him. He'd traveled six hours to spend one night with me in the city. It was quite possible he also loved me. We went up to my apartment for some catching up and then out for dinner at my favorite Italian place. Frankie's was packed with a half-hour wait, but we didn't care. We were in our own world. We clung on to each other in the long line outside.

"Elena?"

I looked up to see two of my friends, Lauren and Cass, a couple.

"Hey!" I ran up to hug them. "Guys, come and meet my boyfriend, Theo." It was the first time I'd said the word aloud to them. *Boyfriend.*

"Okay!"

The four of us chatted until it was our turn for a table. The girls were on their way home to take a crack at cooking a turkey.

"We were both craving Thanksgiving dinner, so we decided it doesn't have to be Thanksgiving to eat our favorite meal. Theo, here's a question for you: How do we get it to cook all the way through without drying out? That's always the biggest challenge."

"First of all," he said, excited to assist, "you have to do away with tradition. Let go of the idea of cooking the whole bird in one piece. Your best bet is to separate the breasts from the thighs." At that, I cringed, and Cass and I shared a private giggle. "The thighs take longer to cook, so put those in first."

"Oh, great idea. I've never thought of that. Hey, he's handy," Lauren said.

"He's alright," I replied, pushing a stray hair from Theo's eyes.

"Well, we're off. It was so nice meeting you!" They turned to leave, and Lauren hugged me and whispered, "So cute. Love the freckles."

The host called our name and led us inside to a table at the back of the restaurant.

"That was fun. I wish you could meet Megan, too, but she left for a solo trip to Thailand, and who knows when she'll be back."

Theo and I sat down to a basket of warm bread and a bowl of mixed olives. It was hard to focus on the menu when all I wanted to do was hold his hands. They were so beautiful; scarred from the kitchen but soft. When the waiter came around, I scrambled to place our order. It helped that I knew the menu by heart.

"One of each of the crostini, except for the one with anchovies."

"Why not? I love anchovies," Theo said.

"Okay, include that one. And the fennel grapefruit salad, sweet potato gnocchi, rigatoni with mini-meatballs, and a bottle of your favorite red." I looked at Theo. "I'm treating."

We sat there staring at each other, looking like those people I hate when I'm feeling lonely. Two smiling idiots. The waiter returned with a bottle of nebbiolo, which he poured for me to taste. I never really know how you're supposed to taste wine, so I swirled it around a little, spilling some on myself as I always do, took a sip, and nodded.

"To surprises," I said, raising my glass.

"To surprises."

The food was perfect, as usual. The lighting was perfect. Theo, sitting across from me with one hand on mine and his fork in the other, was perfect.

And then . . .

"So there's something I want to talk to you about," he said, leaning in closer to me.

I knew it was too good to be true. I slid my hand out from under his, anticipating bad news. He grabbed my fingers and looked down at them, tracing the creases of my knuckles.

"When I left my job in New York to work on the Vineyard this summer," Theo continued, "I set something in motion, a possibility. And it looks like it's going to come through."

I exhaled.

"I am most likely going to Paris for six months for a cooking internship. Plans are still in the works, but it looks like it will happen. I've had this dream of cooking in Paris for a long, long time. I just never imagined I would be leaving someone behind."

I looked around. Frankie's was packed, as always. The couple across from us was sharing an order of tiramisu. A leaf floated down from the plant hanging above our table. A baby protested as it was passed across a table from mother to father, inconsolable, even in the face of the boob. It didn't want to eat or sleep or be held. If only it knew, I thought. That's all I wanted to do. I wanted to eat with Theo, sleep with Theo, and be held by Theo. And now he was going away.

"That kid has no idea how good he has it," I said. Theo smiled but was silent, clearly awaiting a reply. "Listen," I said, flipping his hand over and rolling mine into a fist that fit right in his palm. "I am so excited for you. And as much as I hate that you're leaving, I wouldn't like you so much if you canceled your trip for me. I like that you are pursuing your dream. Anyway," I said, sitting upright and picking up my fork again, "I'm totally coming to visit." I took a big bite of gnocchi.

Theo grabbed my face with both hands, pulled me into a kiss, and then thrust his fist into the air in celebration. "Yes!"

Everyone turned to look at us.

"Congratulations!" I said, holding up my glass again. "I am so happy for you."

We clinked glasses, finished our meal, and ordered dessert. Theo told me all about the Paris possibility—how he felt burned out on New York, how he had always wanted to learn French cooking technique, and how his chef was trying to line something up for him. I was disappointed that he might be leaving just when he was scheduled to return to New York. But it was Paris. A sane person couldn't argue with that. And I was pretending to be sane.

"Oh, I almost forgot," I said in between bites of ricotta cheesecake. "My brother is deejaying tonight, and we have to go. It's his first gig since the accident."

We grabbed a cab and made it just in time for my brother's set. He glided into the room on his crutches and leaned them against the table, balancing à la flamingo on one foot.

"I'm guessing he's the one that looks just like you."

"Yep." I was grinning with big sister pride.

I danced through the entire set. It was impossible not to. I felt like I might implode if I didn't express my joy somehow. Afterward, I escorted Theo backstage to introduce him to my brother.

"Little brother!"

"Hey big sis!" He was tired. I could see that. It was his first big outing in a while, and it took a lot out of him. But he loves to play music more than anything, so I could see the joy emanating from him, too. I gave him a big hug.

"David, this is Theo." They shook hands. I'd told my brother a little bit about Theo, but he hadn't been super-eager to hear about yet another guy. At that point he trusted my judgment less than ever before (with good reason). I didn't have the best track record, and I knew that my description of Theo might sound just like every other guy I'd dated who seemed good at first. So I didn't talk to my brother very much about Theo and instead let their meeting speak for itself.

"Yo, man, that was awesome," Theo said, beaming. It

was funny to hear him in guy mode; his voice slightly lower, a hint of an East Harlem accent.

"Thanks, yeah. I had a lot of fun."

They talked while I caught up with a friend. When Theo left for the restroom, I couldn't resist digging for the verdict.

"So?" I asked my brother, trying to seem casual.

"Yes?"

"What do you think?"

My brother looked at me blankly.

"Of Theo?" I said, growing impatient.

"Why does it matter what I think?" My brother was born with a smirk on his face. He'd always known how to provoke me.

"David, just tell me!"

"Isn't it more important what you think of him?"

"I really like him. A lot," I said. "He treats me like a queen. He is always, always nice to me. And he made me salsa from scratch!"

My brother's friend interrupted us to talk to him. After two minutes of chatting about the sound system, I tapped my brother on the shoulder. He kept nodding to his friend and then looked at me and smiled and said, "I like him, too."

JUST AS THEO'S work at the inn came to a close, his plans for Paris went through. This meant he had one month to spend in New York, with me. I prepared my apartment for his arrival, feigning to be someone who does not keep her clothes in a pile in the closet. I hung each dress, T-shirt, and sweater and placed my shoes in a row, amazed that everything did actually fit in my closet if it was in fact arranged neatly. *I am going to keep it like this from now on.*

I was spending one more weekend on the Vineyard with Theo before bringing him back home. I made the trek up with my brother, who was visiting a friend. Upon arriving at Theo's house, I promptly realized what lay ahead of me. He had a list of all the things he'd have to do to close up the house taped to the wall:

- All windows shut
- Clean sheets
- Newspaper and cloves on mattresses
- Pick up dry cleaning
- Lawn chairs in basement
- Return DVDs to Chilmark Library
- Turn off gas

And the list went on. I tried to hide my doubt that he could complete everything in the little time he had left—twenty-seven hours to be exact, if you allotted time to sleep. I got to work. My brother and his friend lent a hand, too. It was actually kind of fun, our cleaning frenzy. We took breaks now and then to eat everything that wouldn't make the drive home.

At one point I found Theo, screwdriver in hand, looking intently at a dismantled clock.

"What are you doing?" I tried to ask in my least accusatory tone.

"This clock has never worked," he said, picking up a gear and holding it up to the light.

"Um, is this really a priority right now?" I tried to sound as perky as possible. "I mean, I didn't see this on your list."

"This will just take a second." He placed the gear back into the gutted clock and went at it with the screwdriver.

I moved on to another task, laughing to myself and wondering if all men get fixated on fixing things or if it was just the Taurus in him.

"Hey baby," I said later from the kitchen when I had finished cleaning out the refrigerator. "Do you want me to pick up your dry cleaning? That can be one more thing to cross off your list."

"No, it's okay, babe. I'll pick it up later when I go to Cronig's to get cloves."

"But that's in the other direction. Why don't you just let me do it?"

"Don't worry, babe. I got it."

And that's when I learned he is stubborn. (Takes one to know one.) I had visions of us tearing across town on our way to catch the ferry, stopping by the dry cleaner to grab his stuff. And guess what happened. Exactly that. Except that when we pulled into the parking lot, the dry cleaner had just closed. Theo, deflated, tapped on the window, willing someone to open the door. No one came and he was crushed, leaving his favorite sweater behind; the one I had gotten for him, his first gift from me. *Note to self: Sometimes I'm right, too.*

PLAYING HOUSE IN my apartment was fun. Theo cooked for me and did my laundry. Each morning I'd wake up first and make us tea, which he'd sip from bed, watching me as I got ready for work. It was weird being witnessed after having grown so accustomed to living alone with my quirky routines. If Theo found it odd that I changed my outfit four times each morning before leaving the house, he didn't say so. He just sat up in bed smiling and reading *New York Times* restaurant reviews.

Time flew by like this. I'd return home from work. We'd eat something delicious he'd cooked up, like steak and broccoli with buttery turnip puree. We'd watch a movie or walk to the ice cream place up the street. I'd wake up and make us tea. He'd read and sometimes say, "Babe, there's a new restaurant I think you'd really like. We should try it out this week."

And suddenly we were riding the train together, and that evening he'd be leaving for Paris. He was only going for six months, which in New York time is the blink of an eye, but when you're in those first stages of blissed-out, sleepless delirium in a new relationship, six months sucks. I tried to hold it together on the train, but as we approached my stop for work,

I teared up. Theo pulled me into a hug and kissed the top of my head. When I got home from work that evening, he was boarding his plane. I ordered in pumpkin curry.

AT FIRST, WITHOUT Theo's sweet presence in my everyday life, I was limp prey in the face of all my fears. What if he meets a sexy French pastry chef? Or a younger Italian woman? What if, what if, what if? But it was good for me, because I found the more I let the old tapes run on repeat, the more they sounded outdated. Do they even make cassette players anymore? Once I turned off the background noise, I could hear my own voice. And it was the voice of a strong, independent, confident woman. With each day that passed while Theo was in Paris, I put more focus on my own life, on what fulfills me. I joined a new yoga studio, enrolled in some art classes, and kept my closet clean (sort of). We talked online when possible, which, due to the time difference, wasn't as often as either of us would have liked. Every week I would receive a long email in which he'd recap the events of his week and remind me how often he thought of me ("constantly"). I would print out his emails at work and reread them on the train, on my way to painting class. Then I would fold the paper up, stuff it into my bag, and try to suppress smiles all the way to my stop. Gradually I developed a fondness for the space between us, the way it seemed to nearly pulsate with life—our bond like one of the wooden suspension bridges over the dunes on

Martha's Vineyard, pliant enough to bend with our weight but taut enough to hold us. And so together we walked our own paths and counted down days to my visit.

TWO MONTHS LATER . . .

My closet was overflowing. I'd torn dress after dress off the hangers, fussing over which outfit to wear. Balanced on one leg, I shoved the pile of clothes back in with my knee and slid the door shut. I'd be going straight from work to meet The German Girl for dinner and had settled on a sexy dress that tiptoed the line between office and date appropriate. *But it's not a date, Elena.* In a kitchen across the Atlantic, Theo was in his blue bandana, head down, chopping. I'd witnessed him wielding a knife. He could cut onions into translucent, paper-thin slices, his wrist a blur, the knife dancing across the butcher block in a rhythm consistent with his personality: steady. I continued to receive his weekly emails and to fall asleep every night thinking of him.

And then there was The German Girl, who had called me out of the blue, leaving me a voice mail message: "Hi Elena, it's Annika. From Paige's party? I'm sorry it's been forever, but I would love it if you would call me back so I can make it up to you. Dinner, my treat? I hope you don't hate me. But if you do, call me anyway, okay?" I pulled on my boots and grabbed my keys, which I'd taken to keeping in a basket on my dresser. The elevator was playing "Let's Go Crazy" by Prince. Annika was first to reach the restaurant and had set up shop in a dimly lit booth. She was sipping a glass of champagne.

"Wow, you look beautiful," I said. She was wearing one of her strappy designs. Swirls of black velvet outlined her golden shoulders, and her long silky hair looked even fuller than before. It glimmered in the candlelight.

"I do not. You? Elena, I can't even look at you," she said, blushing and hiding her face in her hands. We perused the menu for some appetizers to share.

"Look," Annika said, reaching her hand across the table and placing it on mine. "I'm really sorry I disappeared like that and didn't return your calls. Things were pretty crazy for me back then."

"It's okay," I said, settling into my seat, relaxing.

"Right after I met you, I found out I was pregnant."

I gasped a little and broke into a sweat. I slid out of my sweater slowly, absorbing the shock.

"Is it mine?" I asked.

Annika laughed.

"I had a girl. Her name is June."

I took a big gulp of my water, unfolded my napkin, and placed it on my lap.

"But if you wanted to name her after me, she would have to be December."

Over a bottle of wine and some semolina gnocchi, we caught up on the several months since we'd met. Annika explained that things hadn't worked out with June's father and that she had decided to have June and raise her on her own, along with the help of her closest friend, Karoline. And I told her all about Theo.

"Why did you have to go and get a boyfriend?" Annika asked, tilting her head.

"Because you never called back."

After dinner she walked me to the subway station.

"Elena, I had such a nice time with you tonight. Can we please do this again soon?"

I made a face like I was hesitant, and she tugged me toward her, pulled me into a hug, and kissed my neck.

"Okay, great!" she said, and threw her hand up to hail a cab.

The subway car home was a circus, complete with live music, a break-dance act, and me juggling thoughts of Theo with Annika's dizzying kiss.

"WHATEVER YOU DO, don't mess things up with Theo." TJ stabbed her fork into my ravioli and stole a huge bite. "I like him. He picks on you even more than I do. And he cooks."

"Must you hold your fork like that?" I asked, sliding my bowl farther away from her.

"Like what?"

"Like a kindergartener holds a crayon. You don't have to wrap your whole fist around it."

"Don't change the subject. Look, why don't you talk to him about it? Hell, he'll probably think it's hot, the thought of you with another woman."

"It's not like that," I said, recalling when I'd told Theo that I'd dated women before him. He was the first guy to respond in what I consider the appropriate, nonmoronic way. He wasn't wowed. He wasn't shocked. And he didn't ask to have a threesome.

"I'll figure it out, don't worry."

"Oh, I worry," TJ said, grabbing my glass and stealing the last sip of my wine.

AS MUCH AS I loved Theo, I couldn't help comparing my relationship with him to having a girlfriend. And there were certain aspects of the latter I preferred. In the short time Theo had stayed at my place before leaving for Paris, I had learned there would be things to adjust to—like endless shavings of facial hair scattered around the sink and dirty socks in the kitchen.

A few days later, Annika invited me over to her house. I rang the bell, bearing a box of cupcakes. She opened the door, saying, "Shh," and I followed her on tiptoe down the hallway. She stopped by June's room to give me a glimpse of her sleeping. From the doorway, I watched the pink blanket rise and fall with each tiny breath.

"She's so precious," I said when I joined Annika on the couch in the living room.

"Yeah, she is now. But you weren't here for my two hours of singing, bouncing, and twirling around to get her to stop crying. Do you know what that does to a woman?"

"I don't. But I'm guessing you need a cupcake," I said, handing her one.

After we'd polished off half the box and two pots of tea (all the while stifling laughter so as not to wake June), I returned from clogging the toilet of her clean bathroom to find Annika curled up on the far edge of the couch. She had her knees pulled in toward her, and she looked nervous. I suddenly felt nervous, too. I plopped myself down at the opposite end, letting my legs dangle toward the floor, where I was staring. The air grew thick with awkward silence.

"Maybe I should go," I said softly.

"Elena, don't go. I want to talk to you about something." Annika sat up against the pillows in her corner of the couch. "I've been thinking since our dinner together. I know you are with Theo now, and I am so happy for you. So I don't want to create any confusion for you. From what little I know you, already I think you are amazing. I would like to have you in my life, in whatever way possible. I would very much like to be your friend." I took a moment to digest what she'd said. And then I smiled, feeling relieved.

"Sounds like a plan."

I'd already given the topic plenty of thought. Annika was beautiful, funny, warm, and kind. And Theo was also all those things. But he had stood by me from the very start. He'd rushed into my life with arms wide open, excited and eager to love me. It was Theo who had my heart.

THE DAY BEFORE I was to leave for a trip to visit Theo in Paris, I received an SOS text from TJ.

"Jackass, you're my hero," she said when I met her outside her house. "I've had the worst day."

"What happened?" I asked, handing her my set of *30 Rock* DVDs and her spare set of keys. "Did you mess things up with Antonella already?"

"No, no," she said, unlocking the door. "Things with her are great. In fact, this is all her fault. I had this grand plan of surprising her with her own personalized helmet tonight."

"Her own what now?"

"Her own motorcycle helmet. You know, with her initials painted on the side of it. In gold. It's her favorite color."

"Okay, you are officially whipped."

"I know. Shut up. Anyway, I was in a supergood mood on my way to pick it up on my bike. It was going to be an awesome day. But then it started to rain, so I came back. And then, as you know, I got locked out."

"Yeah, speaking of which, you might want to give those spare keys to your girlfriend since I'll be out of town."

"Yeah, maybe."

"Listen, I have to run home and pack. Good luck with

the helmet," I said, leaning in for a hug. "And don't scratch my DVDs while I'm gone."

"Whatever," TJ said, squeezing me too tightly. "You know you're not coming back."

"Don't be ridiculous. Of course I am."

THEO PLANNED TO meet me at the airport, and as my plane made the initial descent into Charles de Gaulle, I panicked. *What if there's no more spark? What if we don't make each other laugh? What if he's wearing the hat I hate?* As my plane pulled into the gate, my heart pounded in my chest. I tried not to worry and to focus instead on the thought of fresh croissants. With my Italian passport, I breezed through customs. I crossed through the automatic doors to the passenger arrival area. Theo wasn't there yet, which gave me time to get worked up again. Breathe, Elena. I sat down on the cool marble floor and leaned back against the wall, trying to look cool myself.

After an eternity (five minutes), I spied Theo jogging toward me in a jean jacket and the hat I hate. But it didn't matter what he was wearing. My heart did a cartwheel at the sight of him. I jumped up, smiled big, waved, grabbed my bag, and ran toward him, arms out in anticipation of the big embrace. Then I slipped on the slick marble floor in my new UGG boots. My feet flew out from under me. I yelped, flailed, and fell flat on my ass. And we laughed. We laughed and laughed, until Theo, doubled over in hysterics, gathered himself just enough to hobble over and scoop me up into his arms. We clung to each other, hugging and kissing and laughing some more. And then we made our way to the train, Theo carrying my bag on one arm, his other around my shoulder, and me savoring the not one but two croissants he'd brought for me. As we followed the signs for the RER, he walked me through the meal he'd be preparing back at his house, stopping every now and then to kiss the top of my head.

"Goat cheese omelets with bacon and chives." *Smooch.* "Oven-roasted tomatoes." *Smooch.* "French fries, of course. Fromage, charcuterie." *Smooch.* "Pain au chocolat . . ." I wondered how much it might cost to change my return ticket.

In the end, it's not about gender. The question is: Can they cook? (And are they ready to love you?)

# Acknowledgments

Deepest imaginable gratitude for my family, for endless encouragement and unconditional love. I wouldn't be me without you. Mom, thank you for being my biggest fan, for incredibly helpful editing assistance, and for always answering the phone, no matter what time I call. Dad, thank you for instilling in me your hardworking spirit and for having nothing but the utmost faith in me, no matter how many gray hairs I have given you. To my brother, David, thanks for always challenging me to be true to myself, for church laughter, and for hating all my bad boyfriends. To Nonny, thank you for passing on the writer-ly genes and for helping me edit this book. I hope to be as hip as you at age ninety! To Pia and Mau, for immense Italian love and infinite generosity. Thank you for feeding me! Per Sissa, per essere così come sei, creativa, singolare, e unica al mondo. And to Daniela, chi porta gioia ovunque vada.

This book exists because of my agent, Jane Dystel, whose enthusiasm never waned. Thank you for believing in this book, and in me, and for answering all my emails immediately. I don't know how you do it. Thank you also to Miriam Goderich.

To my editor, Krista Lyons, who "got it" right from the start. Thank you for your keen insight and for keeping me on track. And to Brooke Warner, and the rest of the staff of Seal Press, a truly groundbreaking publishing house. The world needs you.

A big "Brilliant!" to my writing teacher, Andrew Craft, without whom creating a book proposal would have seemed like an insurmountable task. To my New York writing buddy, Valerie Reiss, thank you for sharing the vulnerability of the writing process, and more important for the cookies. And to my writing buddy Parisienne, Aurélie Valat. Thank you for having a laugh even louder than mine, so that people glared at you instead. Without you, Paris would be a much colder place.

Enormous thanks to David and Lizzie for a boxful of books, a boatload of encouragement, and for letting me clog your toilet, too.

To my teacher Alex Deschamps, who first encouraged me to write. And to Judy Grahn, Dianne Jenett, Vicki Noble, Kris Brandenburger, and D'vorah Grenn for teaching me to embrace the paradox.

To my friends who read the first drafts: Jane Riley, thank you for supersmart feedback and for seventeen years of friendship. I won't tell anyone you watch *The OC*. To Mary Rohlich, for contagious enthusiasm and die-hard optimism. Nike Clausing, thank you for always begging for more chapters and for being one of the most creative, inspirational women I know. To TG Albert, for years of banter and for talking sense into me now and then. I hate to say it, but sometimes you're right. Deepest thanks and love to Aimee Norwich for years of encouragement and for being brave enough to be an artist. Because of people like you, I find the courage to do it, too.

Thank you to my extended families: La Famiglia Minora and the Eddy-Quintana Clan.

To Sarah Starpoli, my soul. To Ange DiBenedetto, who knows me better than anyone. To Paige Panzner, the funniest Virgo I know. To Gigi Nicolas for "getting" me. To Casey Edwards for demanding that I put more of "me" into my story. To my A.M. ladies: Ricki Grater, Val Andrewlevich, Meghan Dempsey, Rachel Hass, Karen Holmes, Kara Kramer, and Candace Reid. Thank you for being. To Kira Smith for "seeing" me. To Helene and Nikom Los Banos (the wise surf instructor) for your big, big hearts. To Alex Taylor, Wenonah Madison, and the rest of the Aquinnah crew. You're crazy and I love you. To my Right Media and AppNexus peers for years of camaraderie. And to the staff at Spring Restaurant, merci pour les repas à l'oeil et pour le vin à volonté.

Thank you to Nicolas Piégay and the staff at Kooka Boora Café, a little touch of Brooklyn in the Ninth Arrondissement. And to Olivier Galfione at Trini Yoga (not to be confused with The Yoga Teacher). To Jessica Bond and Michelle Snyder: Having good hair helps. To Nick Gwyer for the Joan Collins makeovers. To Alicia Eddy-Quintana for the five-degree photo shoot. To Erica Beckman, photographer extraordinaire of the "I Heart Brooklyn Girls" calendar. To Murray Hill, the hardest-working middle-aged man in show business. And to Bliss Warrior, a trailblazer.

To my fabulous friends who cheered me on: Janice Cummings, Denise Kelly-Simpson, Margie Rothermich, Tina Hernaiz, Baby Juna, Hillary Smith, Natalie Agee, Delano McFarlane, Joanna Lindenbaum, Tif Wolf, Melisse Gelula, Francisco Romero, Meghan Ficca, Patty Jang, Lauren Gutterman, Diana Reilly, Lisa Muñoz, Teresa Soroka, Steve Giacomelli, Theresa Vu, Josh Cohen, Antonella Desini, Cate Newsom, Melody Drummond Hansen, Nat Hansen, Keith DiLauro, Melissa Diamond, Becca Wolff, Lisa Stern, Scrappy, and the Kikibeaks.

And to "Theo." Thank you for following your dream so that I was inspired to quit my high-paying job to follow mine, too (and for supporting me in every possible way while I did so). Thank you for believing in me, for loving me so tenderly, and for always scooping me up when I scoot over to you at night, even though I steal the covers.

# About the Author

Elena Azzoni has performed her written and comedic stage work at various venues throughout New York City and the Bay Area. In November 2007, her one-woman show, *This Is the Way I Pray: Confessions of a Yearning Heart on a Sugar High,* received standing ovations each night of its sold-out run at the BAX Theater in Brooklyn. She has also appeared on the Logo channel and in the debut issue of the "I Heart Brooklyn Girls" calendar. Elena received an MFA from New College of California and a BA in women, gender, and sexuality studies from UMASS Amherst. She currently lives in Paris, France. This is her first book.

# Selected Titles from Seal Press

For more than thirty years, Seal Press has published groundbreaking books. By women. For women.

*Just Don't Call Me Ma'am: How I Ditched the South for the Big City, Forgot My Manners, and Managed to Survive My Twenties with (Most of) My Dignity Still Intact,* by Anna Mitchael. $15.95, 978-1-58005-316-7. In this disarmingly funny tale about the choices that add up to be her twentysomething life, Anna Mitchael offers young women comic relief—with the reality check that there's no possible way to hit all of their desired benchmarks on the way to thirty.

*Wanderlust: A Love Affair with Five Continents,* by Elisabeth Eaves. $16.95, 978-1-58005-311-2. A love letter from the author to the places she's visited—and to the spirit of travel itself—that documents her insatiable hunger for the rush of the unfamiliar and the experience of encountering new people and cultures.

*Dear John, I Love Jane: Women Write About Leaving Men for Women,* edited by Candance Walsh and Laura André. $16.95, 978-1-58005-339-6. A timely collection of stories that are sometimes funny and sometimes painful—but always achingly honest—accounts of leaving a man for a woman, and the consequences of making such a choice.

*Kissing Outside the Lines: A True Story of Love and Race and Happily Ever After,* by Diane Farr. $24.95, 978-1-58005-390-7. Actress and columnist Diane Farr's unapologetic, and often hilarious, look at the complexities of interracial/ethnic/religious/what-have-you love.

*Outdated: Why Dating Is Ruining Your Love Life,* by Samhita Mukhopadhyay. $17.00, 978-1-58005-332-7. An intelligent analysis of how and why young people today are rejecting traditional dating and mating pressures—and why they're better off for doing so.

*Valencia,* by Michelle Tea. $14.95, 978-1-58005-238-2. A fast-paced account of one girl's search for love and high times in the dyke world of San Francisco. By turns poetic and frantic, Valencia is a visceral ride through the queer girl underground of the Mission.

## Find Seal Press Online
www.SealPress.com
www.Facebook.com/SealPress
Twitter: @SealPress